NEW CREATURES IN CHRIST

TRUTH PUBLICATIONS, INC.
CEI BOOKSTORE
PO Box 1056, Athens, AL 35612
www.truthbooks.com

word
in the
heart

6:3

New Creatures in Christ

Table of Contents

ISBN 10: 1-58427-305-4

ISBN 13: 978-158427-305-9

First Printing: 2016

A New Responsibility

Lesson Objective: To show that each individual is responsible for his own sins.

MEMORY VERSE

". . . For all have sinned and fall short of the glory of God. . . . For the wages of sin is death, but the gift of God is eternal life in Christ Jesus our Lord" (Romans 3:23; 6:23).

Ever since you were born, added responsibilities have been placed upon you. You began life depending upon your parents to spoon feed you, change your clothes, and move you wherever you needed to go. Now, you dress yourself, feed yourself, and walk around by yourself. As your abilities increased, so did your responsibilities. You are now responsible for many chores around the house (washing dishes, mowing the lawn, making your bed, etc.).

Even as this is true with regard to physical duties, likewise, you have grown up enough to begin to accept spiritual responsibilities. These responsibilities need our attention and discussion.

The Responsibility Is Yours

By now, sin has entered the life of each of you. Sin is unrighteousness or the disobedience of God's law (1 John 3:4; 5:17). Every individual is guilty of sin, just as Paul said in Romans 3:23, "for all have sinned and fall short of the glory of God."

If each of us is honest with himself, he must confess that he is guilty of sin. Some might have to confess, "I lied to mother"; another might have to say, "I cheated on a test"; or, still another might be forced to admit, "I shoplifted at the mall." But, whatever it is in your case, each one of us is guilty of sin.

Sin has punishment. Paul said, "*For the wages of sin is death*; but the gift of God is eternal life through Jesus Christ our Lord" (Rom. 6:23). The "death" which is the "wages of sin" is eternal condemnation in hell (Rev. 20:15; 21:8). Unless you have had your sins remitted or forgiven, hell awaits you—a sinner before God.

The responsibility for your sins is your own. Mom and Dad can not assume the responsibility for your sins. Only one is responsible for your sins—YOU! Fill in the blanks of this verse which shows that you are the only one responsible for your sins:

"The _____ who _____ shall _____.

The _____ shall not bear the _____ of the _____, nor the _____ bear the guilt of the _____. The righteousness of the righteous shall be upon himself, and the _____ of the _____ shall be upon himself" (Ezek. 18:20).

Now re-read the verse with the blanks filled in to see that the one sinning is the one who suffers for the sins he has committed.

Excuses, Excuses

Almost without exception, when someone condemns us for something, we begin to make excuses. Adam and Eve did the same thing in the Garden of Eden.

God asked Adam, "Have you eaten from the tree of which I commanded you that you should not eat?" (Gen. 3:11). Rather than confessing his guilt, Adam said, "The woman whom You gave to be with me, she gave me of the tree, and I ate" (Gen. 3:12).

God then turned to the woman and said, "What is this you has done?" Eve replied, "The serpent deceived me and I ate" (Gen. 3:13). However, despite the excuses which Adam and Eve offered, punishment was given to each of them because they had committed sins against God. These excuses might have sounded good to other men, but they did not lead to forgiveness. No number of excuses will remove the guilt of sin.

Some Areas of Responsibility

1. Your words. Every word which you speak will be remembered by God on judgment day. Jesus said that "every idle word men may speak, they will give account of it in the day of judgment. For by your words you will be justified, and by your words you will be condemned" (Matt. 12:36, 37).

Most of you are at the age when boys begin to curse and tell dirty jokes. Remember that God will not forget what you said and heard. "Therefore whatever you have spoken in the dark will be heard in the light, and what you have spoken in the ear in inner rooms will be proclaimed on the housetops" (Luke 12:3).

Just because your parents do not know what you say to your friends, does not mean God does not know. What you say can cause you to go to hell.

2. Your actions. Things which you do will also be remembered by God. When you lose your temper and hit someone or say something wrong in hatred, you have sinned. Paul said that one should "be angry and sin not" (Eph. 4:26).

Things you fail to do will also be remembered by God. Do you study the Bible? Do you pray? James said, "Therefore, to him who knows to do good and does not do it, to him it is sin" (Jas. 4:17).

3. Your thoughts. Not only what you say and do, but also what you think is open to God's sight. Hatred of someone in the heart and love of some type of sin are both seen by God. Notice how everything we do or think is open to God's view:

"For the _____ of God is living and powerful, and _____ than any two-edged _____, piercing even to the division of _____ and _____, and of joints and marrow, and is a discerner of the _____ and _____ of the heart. And there is no _____ hidden from His sight, but _____ things are naked and _____ to the eyes of Him to whom we must give account" (Heb. 4:12-13).

Conclusion

Everything we have done in our life is open to God's sight. He sees every sin we have committed. We cannot sin with impunity. God knows our sins and will hold us accountable in judgment for them.

Every sinner is responsible for his own sins. The punishment for sins is eternal damnation in hell. You should begin now to obey God, while you are still young. Years ago Solomon said, "Remember now your Creator in the days of your youth. . . ." You must begin to accept the responsibility for your sins today in order to avoid being cast into hell.

Our God does not want any of us to be destroyed in hell. Therefore, He has provided a means of escape from the punishments of sin. We shall discuss the means of escaping sin's punishments in future lessons.

Student Activity

Thought Questions

1. Suzie and Jason are brother and sister. Jason accidentally broke Suzie's new ipod, so Suzie broke Jason's video game. Jason got mad and slapped Suzie for doing this. Was any sin involved? If so, who sinned and what did they do that was wrong? _____

   _____

   _____

2. Anthony is in the sixth grade. Recently, the boys who get together during recess tell dirty jokes. If Anthony does not tell jokes with the other boys or at least laugh at their dirty jokes, all the guys will dislike him. What should Anthony do? Will he sin if he tells dirty jokes? Will he be sinning if he listens to them and laughs when they laugh?_____

   _____

   _____

   _____

Multiple Choice

_____ 1. A person is guilty of sin when (a) he reaches 21 years old, (b) he violates God's law, or (c) his mother catches him sinning.

_____ 2. Sin is (a) failure to do what God has commanded us to do, (b) committing acts of unrighteousness, or (c) both of these.

_____ 3. If David stole my ball point pen, I should (a) steal his, (b) overlook it, or (c) go talk to him about it.

_____ 4. Since I am a sinner, if I do not get forgiveness of those sins, (a) I will be punished in hell, (b) mother will be punished in hell, (c) father will be punished in hell, or (d) no one will be punished for my sins.

_____ 5. God knows (a) every word we say, (b) every thing we do, (c) every thought we think, or (d) all of these.

Matching

_____ 1. "Be angry and sin not."　　　　a. Ecclesiastes 12:1

_____ 2. "Nor the father bear the　　　　b. Romans 6:23
guilt of the son."

_____ 3. "For all have sinned, and　　　　c. Ezekiel 18:20
fall short of the glory of God.

_____ 4. "By your words, you shalt be　　　　d. Hebrews 4:12
condemned."

_____ 5. "The wages of sin is death."　　　　e. Ephesians 4:26

_____ 6. "The word of God . . . is a　　　　f. Matthew 12:37
discerner of the thoughts
and intents of the heart."

_____ 7. "Remember now your Creator　　　　g. Romans 3:23
in the days of your youth."

True or False

_____ 1. God forgave Adam and Eve because they had a good excuse for eating of the forbidden fruit.

_____ 2. Every person has committed sins if he is old enough to know right from wrong.

_____ 3. God does not know about the things which I do while away from home.

_____ 4. I will be punished because of my father's sins and he will be punished because of my sins.

_____ 5. God not only knows what I do but also what I think.

The Gospel: God's Saving Power

In our last lesson, we studied that each one of us is guilty of sin and personally responsible for our sins. The Bible teaches us that "all have sinned" (Rom. 3:23). Later, we learned that the "wages of sin is death" (Rom. 6:23). As each of us looked at his own life, he was forced to conclude that he has sinned. Thus, if one must stand before God on the basis of his own merit, his predicament is hopeless. Each of us has sinned and, therefore, deserves eternal torment in hell.

Truly, we must turn to God as our only hope of salvation. We are, indeed, unable to save ourselves.

Some Things Which Cannot Save Us

Rather than facing up to the fact that we are lost and need salvation, some have trusted in the things of this world which cannot save. Here are some things in which men trust:

1. Family name or nationality. When Jesus came to the earth, He found Jews who trusted in the fact that they belonged to the family of Abraham, or were of Jewish nationality, for salvation. He said, "and think not to say within yourselves, We have Abraham to our Father. . ." (Matt. 3:9). Being in Abraham's family did not guarantee salvation. Likewise, just because your parents are Christians does not guarantee your salvation.

2. Money. Other people may feel that their riches will get them through this life and, therefore, feel no need of God. The Psalmist commented on this attitude as follows,: "Those who trust in their wealth And boast in the multitude of their riches, None of them can by any means redeem his brother, Nor give to God a ransom for him—For the redemption of their souls is costly, And it shall cease forever" (Psa. 49:6-8).

3. Power. Because of positions they hold, some men trust in their own power without thought of eternity. No one has enough power to stand against God!

4. Knowledge. With emphasis being placed on education, one needs to realize that worldly wisdom will not save. Knowing English,

Lesson Objective: To show that the gospel is what God uses to save souls.

MEMORY VERSE

"For I am not ashamed of the gospel of Christ, for it is the power of God to salvation for everyone who believes, for the Jew first and also for the Greek" (Romans 1:16).

math, and science does not solve the problem of sin. Paul said, "For since, in the wisdom of God, the world through wisdom did not know God, it pleased God through the foolishness of the message preached to save those who believe" (1 Cor. 1:21).

Christ—the Hope of the World

None of the things listed above can save. Salvation did not originate with man; it came from God, through Jesus. Jesus saves!

But, none of us has spoken to Jesus or personally heard Him speak. How are we to find out what to do to be saved?

The Gospel: God's Saving Power

The Bible contains a record of the life of Jesus and teaching that tells men how to live in order to inherit salvation. Knowing this, Paul could say, "For I am not ashamed of the gospel of Christ: for it is the power of God unto salvation to every one that believeth; to the Jew first, and also to the Greek" (Rom. 1:16).

Paul said that the *gospel is God's saving power*. To explain what he meant, notice some of God's other powers. Water is God's power to quench thirst; food is God's power to satisfy hunger. Likewise, the gospel is God's power to save. It is what God has designed to effect the salvation of man's soul.

Can you imagine a person, with a glass of water in his hand, praying for God to quench his thirst? Yet, many people who hold God's saving power—the gospel—in their hand, ask God to save them.

Here is how the gospel operates to save souls as illustrated by Jesus in the parable of the sower (Luke 8:4-14). He compared the gospel to a seed that is planted in a field. The seed contains the power to grow into a fruit bearing plant. However, the seed must be planted, cultivated, and watered before it will produce fruit. The gospel is like that seed. If it is planted in man's heart, cultivated and watered, it will produce a Christian, a saved person! The gospel is the seed that God uses to grow Christians.

What Is the Gospel?

The Bible states that the gospel is "God's saving power," but what is the "gospel"? The word "gospel" means "good news of victory." With regard to Jesus, the "gospel" is the good news of His victory over sin, death, and the grave which brings to us the hope of eternal life.

The gospel consists of facts to be believed (1 Cor. 15:1-5). Paul said the gospel would save us (1 Cor. 15:2) and then defined the gospel to be the record of Jesus dying for our sins, being buried, and rising from the dead on the third day. Thus, the gospel consists of these facts which one must believe.

The gospel also contains commands which must be obeyed. When Paul spoke of the second coming of Jesus, he said that Jesus would take "vengeance on those who . . . do not obey the gospel of our Lord Jesus Christ" (2 Thess. 1:8). Thus, the gospel contains commands which must be obeyed. Obviously, I cannot list them all of them in this paragraph but here is an example: ". . . repent, and let every one of you be baptized" (Acts 2:38).

The gospel contains promises to be enjoyed. Let me repeat the passage which contained the command to repent and be baptized, this time to notice the promises following obedience to the command:

> . . . Repent, and be baptized every one of you in the name of Jesus Christ *for the remission of sins, and ye shall receive the gift of the Holy Ghost*" (Acts 2:38).

Other promises are in the gospel, chief of which is the promise of eternal life.

Conclusion

We have seen that God will save us through the gospel. The gospel is God's means of drawing men to Him. It is His saving power.

Most of you believe the gospel, but have you obeyed it? One can enjoy the promises in the gospel only if he obeys it. Have you obeyed the gospel?

Student Activity
Matching

_____ 1. The Gospel   a. Jesus died for our sins

_____ 2. A Fact in the Gospel   b. Eternal life

_____ 3. A Command in the gospel   c. Money

_____ 4. A Promise of the gospel   d. God's Saving Power

_____ 5. Something which   e. Repent and be baptized
        cannot save

Complete

Fill in the blanks and then use your answers to complete the crossword puzzle below.

1. "The gospel is the power of _____ unto salvation" (Rom. 1:16).

2. "There is _____ righteous, no, not one: . . . for all have sinned and fall short of the glory of God" (Rom. 3:10, 23).

3. "He who believeth and is baptized will be _____" (Mark 16:15).

4. "I tell you, no; but unless you _____ you will all likewise perish" (Luke 13:3).

5. "For the wages of sin is _____" (Rom. 6:23).

6. ". . .But the gift of God is eternal _____ through Jesus Christ our Lord" (Rom. 6:23).

Crossword Puzzle

Define the word written in the line of blocks under the arrow:

_____

_____

_____

_____

_____

Decode This Message

The column of numbers and letters on the left will serve as your code for filling in the blanks for this exercise. The numbers are listed in the exercise. You are to find the corresponding letter and fill in the blank.

1. The ___ ___ ___ ___ is the ___ ___ ___ ___ of God (Luke 8:11).
   8 22 22 23   4 12 9 23

2. The ___ ___ ___ ___ ___ by ___ ___ ___ ___ ___ ___ knew not
   4 12 9 15 23   4 18 8 23 12 14
   God (1 Cor. 1:21).

3. None of them can by any means ___ ___ ___ ___ ___ ___ his
   9 22 23 22 22 14

   brother nor ___ ___ ___ ___ to God a ___ ___ ___ ___ ___ ___
   20 18 5 22   9 26 13 8 12 14
   for him (Psa. 49:7).

4. I declare to you the ___ ___ ___ ___ ___ ___ . . . by which also
   20 12 8 11 22 15

   you are ___ ___ ___ ___ ___ (1 Cor. 15:1, 2).
   8 26 5 22 23

5. The Lord ___ ___ ___ ___ ___ will be revealed . . . in flaming
   17 22 8 6 8

   ___ ___ ___ ___, taking vengeance on them that . . . do not
   21 18 9 22

   ___ ___ ___ ___ the gospel (2 Thess. 1:7-9).
   12 25 22 2

Now read the message of the numbers by filling in the blanks as follows:

___ ___ ___   ___ ___ ___ ___ ___ ___   ___ ___   ___ ___ ___
7 19 22   20 12 8 11 22 15   18 8   7 19 22

___ ___ ___ ___ ___   ___ ___   ___ ___ ___   ___ ___
11 12 4 22 9   12 21   20 12 23   7 12

___ ___ ___ ___ ___ ___ ___ ___ ___.
8 26 15 5 26 7 18 12 13

1	Z
2	Y
3	X
4	W
5	V
6	U
7	T
8	S
9	R
10	Q
11	P
12	O
13	N
14	M
15	L
16	K
17	J
18	I
19	H
20	G
21	F
22	E
23	D
24	C
25	B
26	A

The New Birth

Lesson Objective:
To explain the "new birth" and show that "newness of life" should follow the new birth. This should be impressed as part of discipleship.

MEMORY VERSE

Jesus answered, "Most assuredly, I say to you, unless one is born of water and the Spirit, he cannot enter the kingdom of God" (John 3:5).

So far, we have learned that each person is guilty of sin and stands condemned before God. However, God has made provisions for our salvation. He has promised to let us have a fresh start in life, to let us start over again as if we had just been born.

The opportunity to have purity and freedom from sin is called "The New Birth." Jesus told Nicodemus when he came to Him at night, "Most assuredly, I say to you, unless one is born again, he cannot see the kingdom of God" (John 3:3).

To be able to "see the kingdom of God" is equivalent to salvation. There are only two spiritual kingdoms. One is the kingdom of Satan and the other is the kingdom of Christ. Each responsible person belongs to one of these kingdoms. When a person becomes a Christian, he is translated from Satan's kingdom into Jesus's kingdom (Col. 1:13-14). Jesus said a person could enter His kingdom only if he had been "born again." Read John 3:1-5.

Nicodemus did not understand what Jesus meant when He said that he needed to be "born again." Obviously, an old man could not go back into his mother's womb. Jesus then explained what He meant. He said, "Most assuredly, I say to you, unless one is born of water and the Spirit, he cannot enter the kingdom of God" (John 3:5).

Born of the Spirit

In order to understand the subject discussed by Jesus, one must understand how birth takes place, since Jesus is making a comparison between a natural birth and a spiritual birth. In order for a child to be born, a man must plant his seed in woman. The woman must conceive the seed. Nine months later a child is born. Notice that birth involves two processes: conception and birth.

In the new birth, a person is begotten of God (1 John 2:28-3:2). That means that God planted the seed; He is the father. The seed which is planted is the word of God (1 Pet. 1:23; Jas. 1:18). Since the Holy Spirit is the one who inspired the word of God, one can be said to be "born of the Spirit."

When the seed is planted and received, this is called "conception." When a person receives and believes the gospel, he has experienced the conception part of the new birth.

Every seed that is planted does not result in conception. Many people hear the gospel but do not receive it. Even among those who believe, not everyone is born again. The one who believes has the right to become a child of God. John said regarding Jesus, "He came to His own, and His own did not receive Him. But as many as received Him, to them He gave the right to become children of God, to those who believe in His name: who were born, not of blood, nor of the will of the flesh, nor of the will of man, but of God" (John 1:11-13). The believer is not yet a child of God.

The birth is not complete at the moment of conception. The birth is complete at the moment the crying infant comes from his mother's womb. The "new birth" involves something besides conception also; it involves more than belief.

Born of Water

The second part of the new birth is the bringing forth. This occurs at baptism. For this reason, the "new birth" is described as being "born of water." The person comes forth from the water a "babe in Christ." Several Scriptures in the New Testament allude to the "new birth" by speaking of the new convert as a "babe" (1 Pet. 2:2; Heb. 5:12-14).

Notice that neither of these two parts of birth may be omitted. The person has not been "born again" until he has been "born of water and the Spirit." A person is not a child of God until he has been baptized!

New Life

New life is the result of the new birth. A person arises from the waters of baptism without sin (Acts 2:38). Now he has a "new life" to live.

The transformation that occurs is compared to Jesus's death, burial, and resurrection in Romans 6:1-7. Be sure to read these verses now. The person who wants "newness of life" must go through a "death, burial, and resurrection."

A person must *die* to sin (v. 2, 6-7). Anything that is dead needs to be *buried*. Paul said, "Therefore, we are buried with him by baptism into death. . ." (Rom. 6:4). But, just like Jesus was raised from the dead in His resurrected body, the one who dies to sin is also *raised from the dead* in newness of life. Verse 4 continues, "that just as Christ was raised from the dead by the glory of the Father, even so we also should walk in newness of life."

Notice what has happened: A person dies to sin, is buried, and arises to walk in newness of life.

That you might be sure that you understand what the death to sin and resurrection to life is, read Ephesians 4:17-32. Here the passage contrasts the old man (v. 22) and the new man (v. 24):

The Old Man	The New Man
1. A liar	1. Speaks truth (v. 25)
2. Sins when angry; holds grudges	2. Does not sin when angry; holds no grudges (vv. 26, 27)
3. Steals	3. Does not steal, but works to help the poor (v. 28)
4. Speaks filthy language	4. Only speaks what is good (v. 29)
5. Bitter, evil speaker (v. 31)	5. Kind, tender-hearted, forgiving (v. 32).

The "newness of life" refers to a person's moral change. The "new birth" is the moment that "newness of life" begins.

Since you are guilty of sin, you need to start all over again—to have a fresh start. You need to be "born again." If you ever hope to be saved, "You must be born again." However, do not forget that the person who is born again is expected to walk in newness of life.

Are you ready to take the step into the new birth?

Student Activity
Answer the Following Questions:

1. Who was Nicodemus? _____

_____

2. What does it mean to "walk in newness of life"? _____

_____

3. To what does "born of water" refer?_____

4. How is a person "born of the Spirit"? _____

_____

5. Can one enter the kingdom of God without being baptized? Prove your answer._____

_____

6. How can you tell by Romans 6:4 if baptism is sprinkling, pouring, or immersion? _____

Old Man or New Man?

Instructions: Below are two spaces. Over one space is written "old man" and over the other is written "new man." Below that are thirteen different things listed which people sometimes do. You should determine if each one should be done by the "old man of sin" or the one walking in "newness of life." Read each one and then put the number of that item into the space where it belongs. For example, if number 14 were "murdering your teacher," you should put "14" in the space of "old man."

Old Man	New Man

1. Cheating on a test.

2. Showing respect to one's parents.

3. Making friends with a person no one likes.

4. Using filthy language.

5. Studying your Bible lesson.

6. Helping with the work at home.

7. Beating up kids smaller than you.

8. Reading books with dirty pictures.

9. Talking to someone about his need for salvation.

10. Playing ping pong.

11. Smoking.

12. Watching a football game.

13. Writing on your school desk.

Thought Questions:

1. Judy goes to the Baptist Church. She wanted to be "born again." Her preacher told her that when "she would accept Jesus as her personal Savior," she would instantly be born again. Judy then replied, "I believe Jesus is my personal Savior." Was she born again? _____

_____

_____

2. John claims to have been "born again." However, John reads filthy magazines, smokes, curses, and cheats. What has John failed to do? _____

_____

_____

What Conversion Means

Have you ever had a "darp"? You are probably asking yourself, "What is a 'darp'?" Obviously, you cannot answer the question until you know what a "darp" is. Actually, "darp" is just a word which I made up.

Have you ever been "converted"? How can you answer that until you know what "conversion" is and what is involved in it. Does the word "convert" mean the same to you as the word "darp"? We will begin this lesson by defining the word "convert," but first, notice our memory verse to see how essential it is that every person be converted. A person cannot enter the kingdom of heaven unless he has been converted. Therefore, we need to pay close attention to this lesson.

Definition of "Convert"

The word "convert" comes from a Greek word which means "to turn." It can be used to refer to something becoming good or evil depending upon what a person turns toward.

When it is used with regard to conversion to God or Christ, we mean "the turning of the whole man from the love and practice of sin to the love and service of God." You will notice as we go through this lesson that "conversion" involves a change of heart, life, and relationship. Now let us study the things involved in conversion.

A Change of Heart

When I speak of the "heart" in this lesson, I am not discussing the "blood pump." I am referring to the mind.

A change of heart must occur before one can truly be converted. The change of heart is a change from *unbelief* to *belief*. Notice some of the ones who had a change of heart in the New Testament when they were converted.

1. The people on Pentecost (Acts 2). The Jews to whom Peter preached were the ones who had helped to murder Jesus. When they murdered Him, these Jews felt that Jesus was a blasphemer

Lesson Objective:
To define conversion and show what occurs when a man is converted.

MEMORY VERSE

"Assuredly, I say to you, unless you are converted and become as little children, you will by no means enter the kingdom of heaven" (Matthew 18:3).

and insurrectionist. Peter showed them that He is both Lord and Christ (Acts 2:36). The next verse said that they were "cut to the heart" (v. 37). They had changed their mind about Jesus and felt guilt for murdering the Son of God.

2. Saul (Acts 9:1-22). Saul felt so strongly that Jesus was a "false Christ" that he helped to put Stephen to death for preaching that Jesus was the Christ (Acts 8:1). After that, he went from Jerusalem to Damascus to bring back Christians as prisoners. On the road to Damascus, he saw Jesus in a vision. This changed his mind about Jesus. After that, he believed that Jesus was the Christ, the Son of the living God.

Other examples could be cited, but the real question is, "What do you think about Jesus?" Probably, you believe that He is God's Son, but is He your Lord? If He is really your Lord, you will obey Him. If you have been indifferent to Jesus, you need to change your mind and accept Him as your Lord.

A Change of Life

Many people believe Jesus is the Son of God and state that He is their Savior. However, a change of heart must be accompanied by a change of life. Let us go back to our examples to show what the change of life involves.

1. The Jews on Pentecost (Acts 2). The ones who had murdered Jesus became convinced that Jesus is the Son of God and the Christ (Acts 2:36-37). They wanted to know what they needed to do in order to be saved. Peter told them to "repent and let every one of you be baptized." When I speak of a "change of life," I mean what Peter meant by "repent." This involves putting to death sin in one's life and beginning to live righteously as God wants.

2. Saul (Acts 9:1-22). Saul's life experienced a great change when he was converted. He had to quit persecuting Christians and begin preaching Christ. That was his change of life.

You, too, must have a "change of life." Your life must change just as the life of the ones in the two examples cited above had to change. Your "change of life" might be to quit lying and begin telling the truth, to quit "cutting up" in Bible class and begin seriously to study God's word, or to quit using filthy language and begin speaking only words of purity.

Whatever it will mean in your own life, before you can be converted, you must make a change in life. Put Christ first.

A Change of Relationship

A change of heart and life are no more essential than is the change of relationship. A person guilty of sin is the son of the Devil (John 8:41-44). He must become the son of God in order to be saved.

Galatians 3:26-27 tells us how this change occurs. Here are the verses:

> For you are all sons of God through faith in Christ Jesus. For as many of you as were baptized into Christ have put on Christ.

The Galatians had become children of God by faith in Christ. But how did they do it? The word "for" introduces an explanation of how they became God's children—they were baptized into Christ. This changed their relationship to God. They were "born of water and of the Spirit" and were now sons of God. Therefore, they could call God their Father (Gal. 4:4-7).

Going back to our two examples, we read that both the Pentecostians (Acts 2:38) and Saul (Acts 9:18; 22:16) were baptized. This changed their relationship with God. Let us illustrate the necessity of a change in relationship.

Suppose that a rich man were going to marry a beautiful woman. He was engaged to her and had planned to marry her. On the set date, the couple went to get married. When

the groom stepped out of his car, a diesel truck ran over him and killed him. Would the girl inherit his fortune? No. She was not his wife yet and, therefore, had no claim on his wealth. Her relationship had not changed.

The young lady had a change of heart toward the man. She no longer felt indifferent towards him; she now loved him. She had a change of life. She had quit dating other men in order to date him alone. But her relationship had not changed and, therefore, she did not inherit his fortune.

Likewise, one cannot consider himself an heir of God unless he changes his relationship. He must cease to be the son of the devil and become the son of God. This is done when a person is baptized.

Conclusion

"Assuredly, I say to you, unless you are converted and become as little children, you will by no means enter the kingdom of heaven" (Matt. 18:3).

"Repent therefore and be converted, that your sins may be blotted out. . ." (Acts 3:19).

Have you been converted? If not, you cannot enter the kingdom of heaven. Do not postpone your obedience to Jesus!

Student Activity
True or False

_____ 1. Conversion can occur without one making any changes in his life.

_____ 2. A person is converted the moment he believes.

_____ 3. The "change of heart" which occurs in conversion is the change from unbelief to belief.

_____ 4. Baptism is what causes the change in relationship between man and God to occur.

_____ 5. There is no biblical evidence that Saul repented when he was converted.

Multiple Choice

_____ 1. Which of the following is the Bible method of conversion:
(a) Going to a mourner's bench, (b) Praying through,
(c) Faith only, (d) Baptism in the Holy Spirit, (e) None of
these, (f) All of these.

_____ 2. At which point in conversion does one become a son of
God? (a) When he believes, (b) When he repents, (c)
When he is baptized, (d) When he dies.

_____ 3. In conversion, (a) man does everything to save himself
and God does nothing, (b) God provides the means for
salvation but man must make use of them, (c) God does
everything and man does nothing.

Match the Verse and the Quotation

_____ 1. "For the hearts of this people have grown dull. Their ears
are hard of hearing, And their eyes they have closed,
Lest they should see with their eyes and hear with their
ears, Lest they should understand with their hearts and
turn, So that I should heal them."

_____ 2. "Brethren, if anyone among you wanders from the truth,
and someone turns him back, let him know that he who
turns a sinner from the error of his way will save a soul
from death and cover a multitude of sins."

_____ 3. "Jesus answered, 'Most assuredly, I say to you, unless
one is born of water and the Spirit, he cannot enter the
kingdom of God.'"

_____ 4. "Assuredly, I say to you, unless you are converted and
become as little children, you will by no means enter the
kingdom of heaven."

_____ 5. ""Repent therefore and be converted, that your sins may
be blotted out, so that times of refreshing may come from
the presence of the Lord. . . ."

_____ 6. "For as many of you as were baptized into Christ have
put on Christ."

a. **James 5:19,20**

b. **Matthew 18:3.**

c. **Matthew 13:15.**

d. **Galatians 3:27.**

e. **John 3:5.**

f. **Acts 3:19.**

22

Change of Heart?

Read each passage and see if you can find any evidence of a change of heart, life, and relationship having occurred. Write where you find that evidence in each blank. The first one is done for you.

Scripture	Change of Heart	Change of Live	Change of Relationship
Acts 2:1-47	vv. 36, 37	vv. 38, 41	vv. 38, 41
Acts 8:5-12			
Acts 8:27-40			
Acts 9:1-22			

Class Discussion

1. Quote the memory verse.

2. Define "conversion."

3. Is everyone converted who claims to be? Give reasons for your answer.

4. Do the cases of conversion studied in the above activity follow a pattern? If so, what is the pattern?

Words to Know

"Conversion"—the turning of the whole man from the love and practice of sin to the love and service of God

In Christ: A New Relationship

Thus far in our lessons, we have studied steps that lead one into Christ. We studied conversion or "the new birth" with the intent of showing each person how to become a child of God. Our study now assumes that you are a child of God.

When a baby is born into a family, he enters a relationship with all other members of the family. As a member of the family, the newborn child receives many blessings and privileges, such as love, support (i.e., food, clothing, and shelter), and the right of inheritance. The child must soon assume some responsibilities simply because he is part of this family relationship.

As many as have been "baptized into Christ" (Gal. 3:27) have entered into a new relationship. That new relationship is the object of our study in this lesson.

A New Family Relationship

1. A new relationship to God. The person "born again" is born into the family of God. "Behold what manner of love the Father has bestowed on us, that we should be called children of God!" (1 John 3:1). To say that a person is a child of God indicates that God is his Father.

As a consequence of being a child, one has the privilege of crying unto God, "Father!" (Gal. 4:6). Let us meditate on that privilege for a minute. To the Greeks who lived when Paul wrote his epistles, gods were common and numerous. Not all pagan gods were good. Some were envious of man and vicious to him. But Paul reassured Christians that there is only one God and that He sustains to us a relationship like a Father to a son.

The relationship of father-son is used by Jesus as a basis for praying to God (Matt. 7:9-11). When a son asks his father for a piece of bread, the father does not pick up a rock and say, "Go chew on that for a while." Rather, he gives him good food to eat. Jesus argued that, if we human fathers know how to give good gifts to our children, how much more does the heavenly Father

Lesson Objective:
To describe our new relationship as a result of being "in Christ." In doing this, we desire to give attention to both our privileges and responsibilities.

MEMORY VERSE

"Behold what manner of love the Father has bestowed on us, that we should be called children of God! Therefore the world does not know us, because it did not know Him" (1 John 3:1).

know how to give good gifts to His children? Indeed, with John we stand in awe saying, "Behold what manner of love the Father has bestowed on us, that we should be called children of God!" Those who have not been "born again" have no right to call upon God in prayer as "Our Father in heaven."

2. A new relationship to Christ. Our relationship to Christ is that of brother. That Christ is our brother is evident from the fact that He is the "Son of God" and we are "sons of God." On this fact — that both Jesus and Christians are sons of God—Paul argued, "And if children, then heirs; heirs of God, and joint-heirs with Christ. . ." (Rom. 8:17).

Whatever inheritance awaits Jesus as the Son of God will be shared with us as "joint-heirs" with Christ. The exact nature of that inheritance is beyond our ability to understand. Nevertheless, it awaits the sons of God who are brothers to Christ.

3. A new relationship to one another. As sons of God, we become brothers and sisters in Christ. The term "brother" is used so frequently around the church building that few of us ever meditate on its meaning. Thus, to most of us, "brother" is used in a formal way without thought being given to its meaning.

As brothers and sisters, we need to feel and act toward one another as brothers and sisters in the flesh should act toward each other. We must love one another (1 John 2:9-10). We must help each other when in need (1 John 3:17-18). This responsibility is a part of being in a new relationship with God, Christ, and each other.

A New Citizenship

When a person is converted, he changes his citizenship from the kingdom of Satan to the kingdom of Christ. (Notice that we have changed figures for studying different aspects of your new relationship.) The Christian becomes a fellow-citizen in the kingdom (Eph. 2:19).

Citizens in any kingdom have privileges and responsibilities. A citizen in the United States, for example, has the inalienable rights of freedom of religion, speech, and press. He has the responsibilities of loyalty and paying taxes.

A citizen in God's kingdom has the privilege or blessing of redemption—forgiveness of sins (Col. 1:13-14). He also has responsibilities.

He must serve in Christ's army (2 Tim. 2:3-4; 2 Cor. 10:3-6). We are not fighting a physical battle but a spiritual one, not against flesh and blood but against spiritual wickedness. As a soldier, I must put on the gospel armor (Eph. 6:10-18), and fight militantly against Satan's forces.

As a citizen in Christ's kingdom, I must obey my King—Jesus (Acts 2:30). Any commandment He has uttered, I must obey. Notice my relationship to Jesus, in this figure, is that of king-subject. He is my Lord (Acts 2:36).

Since the kingdom in which the "born again" believers are citizens is the church, let us be sure to understand that our responsibilities in the kingdom are responsibilities discharged in the church. I must, therefore, support the church financially (1 Cor. 16:1-2). I must attend worship (Heb. 10:25). I must sing (Eph. 5:19) and pray (1 Thess. 5:17). Basically, I must support every good work in which the church can scripturally engage.

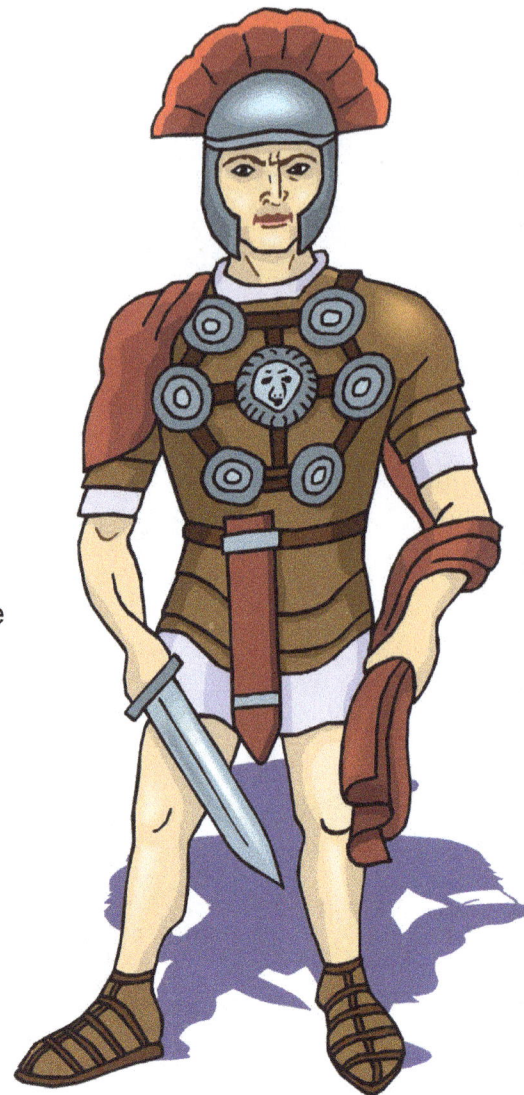

Conclusion

A person who forsakes his responsibilities in the army is a "deserter." So is the person who forsakes his responsibilities as a result of being "in Christ." Many blessings are yours simply because of Christ. Do not forsake the few responsibilities he has given you and lose those blessings. A responsibility comes with every privilege. Your new relationship has given you many blessings and a few responsibilities.

Student Activity

Short Answer

1. Name the privilege which each verse describes as yours because of your new relationship to God.

    a. Acts 2:38 _____

    b. John 14:2 _____

    c. John 16:23, 24 _____

    d. Romans 8:28 _____

    e. 1 Corinthians 6:19, 20 _____

2. Name the responsibility taught in each verse.

    a. Hebrews 10:25 _____

    b. Ephesians 4:22, 23 _____

    c. James 1:26, 27 _____

    d. James 3:8-10 _____

    e. Ephesians 5:19 _____

Fill in the Blanks

In this lesson, we studied the relationship we have in Christ and first compared it to the _____ relationship. In this relationship _____ is compared to our father and Jesus as our _____.

Being a son of God gives a person certain privileges. This was shown when Jesus taught on the subject of _____ that _____ cares for us like a father cares for his son. Being a son of God gives one the right to the _____. We are joint-heirs with _____.

A Secret Message

In this exercise, you will find a long list of letters. Beginning with the first letter, mark out each letter thereafter according to the numbers at the bottom of the exercise. EXAMPLE: Count 6 letters, then mark out the next letter. Count 4 letters and mark out the next letter. (Do not count the marked out letters.) The marked out letters serve as spaces between words. What does the message say?

B E H O L D A W H A T Z M A N N E R B O F Y L O V E C T H E
X FAT H E R D H A S V B E S TOW E D E O N U U S F T H A T T
W E G S H O U L D S B E H C A L L E D R T H E I C H I L D R E N
Q O F J GOD P

6, 4, 6, 2, 4, 3, 6, 3, 8, 2, 2, 4, 2, 6, 2, 6, 3, 8, 2, 3

What does the puzzle say? _____

_____

_____

_____

Thought Questions

1. Contrast the relationship which God has to us as Father-son with the relationship He would have to us if He were our enemy.

2. Compare a soldier in the United States army with a soldier in God's army.

3. Explain how one gets into the family of God. What steps must he take?

4. Does everyone have the right to pray, "Our Father, which art in heaven"? Give reasons for your answer.

The New Life

MEMORY VERSE

"I beseech you therefore, brethren, by the mercies of God, that you present your bodies a living sacrifice, holy, acceptable to God, which is your reasonable service. And do not be conformed to this world, but be transformed by the renewing of your mind, that you may prove what is that good and acceptable and perfect will of God" (Romans 12:1-2).

"Therefore we were buried with Him through baptism into death, that just as Christ was raised from the dead by the glory of the Father, even so we also should walk in newness of life" (Rom. 6:4).

Every person who has been baptized into Christ is expected to make changes in his life. The changes in one's life are so obvious to those around him, that they can see that he is living a new life. His life and goals are different from what they were prior to his baptism.

Romans 12:1-2

No passage in the New Testament discusses the basis of this change in more detail than does our memory verse for this lesson. Read the verses and study them with me:

I beseech you therefore, brethren, by the mercies of God, that you present your bodies a living sacrifice, holy, acceptable to God, which is your reasonable service. And do not be conformed to this world, but be transformed by the renewing of your mind, that you may prove what is that good and acceptable and perfect will of God.

Paul beseeches (begs) the Roman Christians to present their bodies a living sacrifice to God. The basis of his exhortation is "the mercies of God." Paul said, "I beseech you . . . by the mercies of God." What Paul is asking is that these Christians govern their lives in light of all that God's mercy has given to them. God gave us His only Son in sacrifice for our sins. Since God has shown this kind of love for me, I should try to live as He desires. My outward conduct should show my love for Jesus. Jesus said, "If you love Me, keep My commandments" (John 14:15).

Suppose that your neighbor's house caught on fire and that your father rushed into the house to save the man who lived there. Your Dad saved the man but, in doing so, was burned to death by the flames. On the day of his funeral, the neighbor whose house had burned decided to go fishing instead of attending the funeral. What would you feel toward this neighbor? Did he act like he cared that your Father had died in order to save his life? In a similar manner, God gave His Son's life to save you from the fires of hell. These are the "mercies of God" which Paul is asking us to remember so that we will present our bodies a living sacrifice to God.

But what did Paul mean when he asked that Christians "present your bodies a living sacrifice"? To understand this request, a person must understand Jewish sacrifices. The Jews offered animals on a sacrificial altar. The animal had to be one that was in perfect health. When the sacrifice began, the animal was slain and burnt in worship to God.

Paul said that he wanted us to present our bodies in worship of and service to God just like an animal that is used to worship God. However, unlike the dead animal, one's body is a living sacrifice. That is, everything that I do in life is done as worship to God. "Or do you not know that your body is the temple of the Holy Spirit who is in you, whom you have from God, and you are not your own? For you were bought at a price; therefore glorify God in your body and in your spirit, which are God's" (1 Cor. 6:19-20).

Going further into Romans 12:1, 2, we see that Paul tells how to present one's body a living sacrifice to God. First, he tells us what presenting one's body a living sacrifice requires—"Do not be conformed to this world."

Just about everyone feels the pressure to imitate the world. Judy wants to go to the Junior-Senior prom, so she says, "Everybody else in my class is going." The Scriptures forbid "lascivious" conduct, including such things as dancing (Gal. 5:19). The Christian who presents his body as a living sacrifice to God dares to be different. He would prefer to be different in order to please God. So Judy submits her will to God's will and chooses not to attend the prom. Everyone might consider this person "different" but she cares about only one thing—pleasing God. "In regard to these, they think it strange that you do not run with them in the same flood of dissipation, speaking evil of you" (1 Pet. 4:4).

The one who walks in "newness of life" has quit trying to conform to the world. Rather, he has been "transformed by the renewing of your mind." The new life is a life different from the one which existed before conversion. What caused it?

30

Paul said the transformation was caused "by the renewing of your mind." The real change occurred when the individual changed his goals in life. When a decision is to be made, he no longer thinks the following: (1) Will this impress my friends? (2) Will this make everyone like me? (3) Do I like it? (4) What is everyone else doing? Rather, he asks, "What would Jesus want me to do?" and "Will this help me to go to heaven?"

Therefore, his whole life has been transformed because his mind has been renewed.

Romans 6:16-19

This passage also discusses the great change that occurs when an individual obeys the gospel. Verse 19 says, "I speak in human terms because of the weakness of your flesh. For just as you presented your members as slaves of uncleanness, and of lawlessness leading to more lawlessness, so now present your members as slaves of righteousness for holiness." Notice the change Paul pointed out in verse 19. Just as previously the Romans had given their bodies to sin, now they should equally dedicate their bodies to holiness. As diligently as an alcoholic strives to get a drink, a Christian should strive to please God.

Colossians 3:1-4

"Set your mind on things above, not on things on earth." Paul knew what changed conduct. Therefore, he asked that the saints at Colosse change their objects of love. A change of mind would necessarily cause a change of life as he went on to describe in Colossians 3:5-4:6.

Conclusion

What is the nature of the "new life"? The "new life" is a life governed by the desire to please God. When a person decides that pleasing God is his goal, his conduct will change.

"You shall love the Lord your God with all your heart, with all your soul, and with all your mind" (Matt. 22:37). "If you love Me, keep My commandments" (John 14:15).

Student Activity
Problems in Life

Below are some real life situations. On the right, a list of Scripture references appear. Read the story and then pick out the verse which best tells how to act in the situation. Using the verse selected, tell what should be done in each case. Some of the stories will use two Scriptures in solving the problem.

1. Cindy is crying because her father is sick. What should you do?

_____

_____

Scripture: _____

2. John is a Christian. Everyone of his friends curses, smokes, drinks, and cheats. Will this affect him. What should he do?____

_____

Scripture: _____

3. Janie stole Jodi's boyfriend. Jodi is so mad that she decided to get even. She decided to spread an ugly rumor about Janie. What did Jodi do wrong? _____

_____

Scripture: _____

4. Basketball practice is on Wednesday night during church services. David is trying to make the basketball team and, therefore, missed church services to go to basketball practice. Did David sin? If so, what was his sin? _____

_____

Scriptures: _____

5. Lynda is a new girl at school. She is 5 feet, 2 inches tall and weighs 185 pounds. All the boys tease her about her weight. Jeff, a member of the church, did it so much that Lynda began to cry. Did Jeff do anything wrong? If so, what?_____

_____

Scripture: _____

Matthew 7:12

Hebrews 10:25

Romans 12:19-21

Galatians 6:2

Ephesians 4:26

1 Corinthians 15:33

Matthew 6:33

32

True or False

_____ 1. "Newness of life" begins before one is baptized.

_____ 2. Since Jesus gave His life for me, I should try to use my life to serve Him.

_____ 3. The Christian should let his life be governed by how everyone else lives.

_____ 4. The Bible does not contain instructions which will apply to everyday living. It is only a book to be used at church services.

_____ 5. The change of mind is what causes a person to change his conduct.

Thought Questions

1. Jennifer is trying to buy a new dress. The one she has picked out is the perfect color; pink looks precious on her. The dress is the right price. Everyone at school will think that it looks lovely on her. Jennifer knows that the dress is too short and has a plunging neckline but would still like to buy the dress. Read 1 Timothy 2:9-10 and then tell what she should do.

2. Jim just moved to a new school. Since he has no friends there, he wants to make a good impression on everyone so that they will like him. All the boys use filthy language and tell dirty jokes. What should he do?

For Class Discussion

Below are some of the excuses people offer for justifying their conduct. Examine each one in class discussion guided by your teacher.

1. "Everybody else does it."

2. "Nobody will see me."

3. "I must do it to be popular."

4. "If Joe Ned can do it, so can I. He is a Christian."

5. "I want to do it."

The Two Covenants

Nearly 1500 years before Christ, God instituted the religious system of the Jews. He gave specific instructions regarding the manner in which worship was to be conducted. Any deviation from that pattern was sinful and not accepted by God.

One of the requirements of the Mosaical law was that worship was to be offered through a priest. The priest had to be a descendant of the tribe of Levi (Num. 8:14-19; Deut. 17:9; 18:1-5) and the high priest, a descendant of Aaron (Num. 25:10-13). Any sacrificial worship which was offered without the priest displeased God. (In 1 Samuel 13:8-15, Saul was rejected by God as king of Israel because he personally offered the sacrifice to God, instead of a priest.)

All of these commandments were given by divine approval and were expected to be obeyed. This was a very important part of the Mosaical law.

Jesus—Our High Priest

One of the basic facts about Jesus is that He is the High Priest of every Christian (Heb. 3:1; 4:14-16; 8:1). However, Jesus was not a descendant of Levi, but of Judah (Heb. 7:14). If Jesus expected to be a high priest under the Mosaical law, He would not have been able, since He was a descendant of the wrong tribe.

To admit that we have Jesus as our high priest necessitates a change of law. Hebrews 7:12 says, "For the priesthood being changed, of necessity there is also a change of the law." Thus, we come to the main point of this lesson. Jesus had to abolish and fulfill the Mosaical law in order that He could institute a new law.

A Better Covenant

When Jesus changed the law, He improved it; "Jesus became the surety of a better covenant" (Heb. 7:22). Below is a chart that shows the superiority of Jesus's covenant to the Mosaical covenant in certain areas:

Lesson Objective: To show the two covenants in the Bible and that we are under the new covenant, the New Testament.

MEMORY VERSE

"For the priesthood being changed, of necessity there is also a change of the law" (Hebrews 7:12).

Area of Contrast	Mosaical Law	Law of Christ
Sacrifice	Animals	Jesus (Heb. 9:11-14)
Priest	Sons of Levi	Jesus
Number of Offerings	Many; Never Ending (Heb. 10:1-2)	Once for all (Heb. 9:26)
Effect of Offering	No remission of sins (Heb. 10:3, 4)	Remission of sins (Matt. 26:28)

By contrasting these points, we can rejoice along with the author of Hebrews (10:9), that Jesus "takes away the first" (i.e., the Mosaical law), "that He may establish the second" (i.e., the law of Christ).

How thankful each of us should be that we do not have to worship under the Mosaical law. Here is a brief description of Mosaical worship for you to contrast with New Testament worship:

The worshipper brought a goat without blemish which the priest was to offer in sacrifice to God because of sins which the worshipper had committed. The worshipper was expected to bring the goat to the door of the place of worship, lay his hands upon the head of the goat, and kill it. Then the priest came, touched the blood to the altar and then poured the rest of the blood into the basin of the altar. The priest then removed all the fat from the sin-offering and burnt the goat as an offering to God. (Read Lev. 4:27-31.)

No wonder the covenant of Christ is described as a better covenant!

The Old Covenant Was Abolished

The Mosaical covenant was given to only one nation—Israel. Every other nation was outside the covenant and called Gentiles. The Jewish people had no contact with Gentile people because they felt themselves to be superior to other people, since they were recipients of God's special blessings.

In Ephesians 2:11-18, Paul showed that this old distinction was abolished by Christ. Prior to Christ's work, the Gentiles were, indeed, underprivileged when compared to the Jews. Gentiles were (1) separate from Christ, (2) alienated from the commonwealth of Israel, (3) strangers from the covenants of promise, (4) without hope, and (5) without God. But through Christ, these people are brought near to God. How did this happen?

Read Ephesians 2:14-16 to see. Christ broke down the middle wall of partition separating Jews and Gentiles. What was that wall? The Mosaical law! Christ abolished it! By getting rid of the Mosaical law, Christ could reconcile all men, both Jews and Gentiles, to God through the cross.

Implications from This

What difference does this make to you and me? We have already seen that the nature of worship has changed as a direct result of that, but let us notice something else more basic.

Galatians 5:1-5

Paul was writing to some Jewish Christians who had decided to go back to the Mosaical law, the Old Testament, in order to make Gentiles obey the law of circumcision before becoming Christians. Paul, in this passage, shows the results from doing this:

1. Christ is of no profit to the person.

2. The person is debtor to do the whole law (i.e., if a person wants to obey part of the Old Testament, he must obey all of it).

3. He is severed from Christ.

4. He is fallen from grace.

Practically, what this means to us is that we must not go to the Old Testament in authorizing our religious practices. Suppose that I wanted to go back to the Old Testament to teach that one should offer animal sacrifices in worship to God. To do so would mean that I was obligated to keep the entire Old Testament and not just a part of it. It would mean that everything for which Christ came to the earth was useless because I had decided that the way it was before He came was better. To do this meant that I had thrown away my hope of salvation through Christ and was, therefore, fallen from grace.

Thus, we each need to learn the lesson that we are not living under the Old Testament law but under the law of Christ. Consequently, we cannot appeal to the Old Testament for religious authority. We must confine ourselves to the New Testament.

Student Activity

Unscramble the Message:

In the exercise below is a message for you to unscramble. Using the code given, write out the message:

A = 26	B = 25	C = 24	D = 23	E = 22
F = 21	G = 20	H = 19	I = 18	J =17
K = 16	L =15	M=14	N= 13	O= 12
P= 11	Q= 10	R = 9	S= 8	T= 7
U= 6	V=5	W=4	X= 3	Y=2
Z= 1	Space = *	Period = #	Comma =!	

21 12 9   *   7 19 22   *   11 9 18 22 8 7 19

12 12 23   *   25 22 18 13 20   *   24 19 26 13 20

22 23 !   *   7 19 22 9 22   *   18 8   *   14 26

23 22   *   12 21   *   13 22 24 22 8 8 18 7 2

*   26   *   24 19 26 13 20 22   *   26 15 8 12   *

12 21   *   7 19 22   *   15 26 4 #

From what is written in the coded question, answer the following question: Why did the law have to be changed? _____

_____

_____

Short Answer Questions:

1. Since the Old Testament is not binding on us today, some wonder why anyone should read it. Read the verses listed below and tell what use the Old Testament has for us today.

   a. 1 Corinthians 10:6, 11 _____

b. Romans 15:4 _____

c. John 5:39 _____

2. Using Galatians 5:1-5, name the four things Paul said would occur if one returned to the Mosaical law for authority.

a. _____

b. _____

c. _____

d. _____

3. When did Christ's law go into force (read Heb. 9:15-17 for the answer)? _____

4. Name any three Mosaical laws not binding on Christians:

a. _____

b. _____

c. _____

5. Are Christians to observe the Ten Commandments recorded in Exodus 20? _____ If not, does that mean that Christians can steal, kill, and commit adultery? _____ Why or why not? _____

Can You Be of Any Help?

1. David and Cathy were discussing whether the church should use instrumental music in songs of worship to God. Cathy said that there is no authority for instrumental music. David replied that Psalm 150:3-5 commands us to praise God on musical instruments. Can you give Cathy some advice on what she should tell David?

2. The church where Suzie attends sent her a letter telling her that they expected her to tithe to God. Enclosed were some envelopes for her to use in mailing in her tithes. Will you help Suzie to find out if she is supposed to tithe under the law of Christ? (You will probably need to check in a concordance under "Tithe" to see if the New Testament commands Christians to tithe.)

38

3. Robert goes to the Seventh Day Adventist Church. He is trying to convince Oscar that he must observe Saturday, the Sabbath Day, in worship to God. Will you see what you can find out about worshipping on Saturday or observing the Sabbath so that you can take part in their discussion?

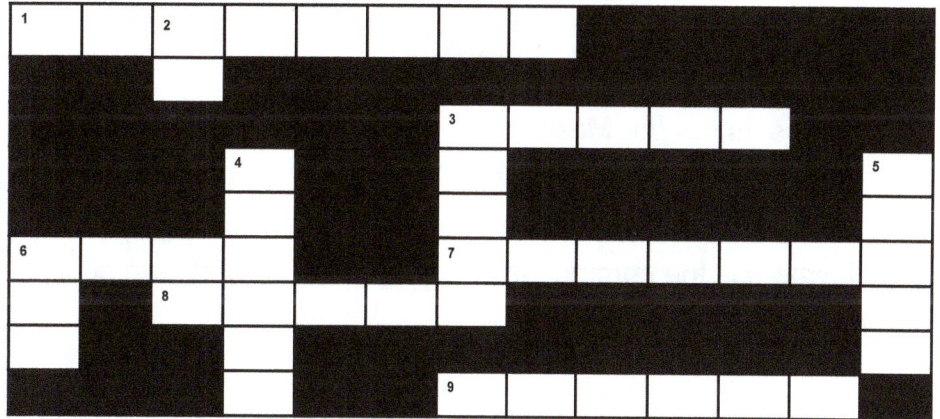

A Crossword Puzzle for You

Across

1. Which people were not in covenant relationship with God before Christ came, Jews or Gentiles?

3. Who is our High Priest today?

6. From which tribe did the priests descend under the Mosaical law?

7. What was offered in sacrifice to God under the Mosaical law?

8. When did Jesus's law go into effect? At His

9. Under which law did the sacrifice make possible the remission of sins, the law of Moses or the law of Christ?

Down

2. Could Jesus have been a priest under the Mosaical law?

3. From which of the twelve Israelite tribes did Jesus descend?

4. Who offered the sacrifice under the Mosaical law? The

5. What was offered in sacrifice to God under the law of Christ?

6. What had to be changed in order for Jesus to be a priest? The

_____.

A New Day of Worship

Our last lesson demonstrated that the Mosaical law was replaced by the law of Christ. This lesson will build on the foundation that was laid in that lesson. We learned that the old law was abolished and replaced by a new law. Now we shall notice some results from that fact.

The Jews, under the Mosaical law, worshipped on the Sabbath, the seventh day of the week (Exod. 20:8-11). The commandment to observe the Sabbath day was only given to Israel (Deut. 5:1-5, 12-15). Nowhere is the commandment to observe the Sabbath given to non-Israelites.

The following were commandments given for observance on that day:

Lesson Objective:
To show that the day of worship changed when the law was changed and that Christians are to observe the Lord's Day.

HOW IT WAS TO BE OBSERVED	PUNISHMENT FOR DISOBEDIENCE
1. Do not work (Exod. 31:15) 2. Do not kindle fire (Exod. 35:3) 3. Do not gather sticks (Num. 15:32-36) 4. Offer burnt offerings (Num. 28:9-10) 5. Do not buy goods (Neh. 10:31; 13:15-18) 6. Do not bear a burden (Jer. 17:21) 7. Prepare shewbread (1 Chron. 9:32) 8. A person must stay at his place (Exod. 16:29).	D E A T H (Exod. 31:14: Num. 15:32-36)

Although some churches claim to believe in observing the Sabbath, none of them obeys all of the commandments given with regard to how to observe the day and not one of them would dare to try to enforce the Old Testament's instructions for punishing the ones who did not properly observe the Sabbath.

In Colossians 2:14-17, Paul affirmed that Jesus had abolished and replaced the Old Testament by nailing the old law to the cross.

MEMORY VERSE

"Now on the first day of the week, when the disciples came together to break bread, Paul, ready to depart the next day, spoke to them and continued his message until midnight" (Acts 20:7).

The argument continued in v. 16 in which Paul stated some results from the fact that the old law was abolished. He said, "Let no man therefore judge you . . . regarding . . . sabbaths."

Since the worship on the Sabbath day was abolished, we must now examine the New Testament to see if any worship of any type was mentioned on any day. In looking through the New Testament, we find reference to only one day as being specifically set aside for New Testament worship.

The Lord's Day

Here are some evidences that the New Testament church worshipped on the first day of the week:

1. Acts 20:7. Rather than looking at this verse alone, look at its context. Paul left Philippi by ship and sailed for five days before arriving at Troas. There he had to wait seven days in order to meet with the church. Evidently, Paul arrived in Troas late on Sunday or early on Monday. However, he knew that on Sunday the church would meet, so he waited there until services were over and then left for Assos.

2. 1 Corinthians 16:1-2. In these verses, Paul commanded that Christians give on the first day of the week. Evidently some gathering occurred on this day at which this command could be obeyed.

On the basis of this evidence and the evidence from secular writers of the same period, church historians are agreed that the early church assembled and worshipped on Sunday. This is the day that is called the "Lord's Day" (Rev. 1:10), because it was on this day that (1) Jesus arose from the dead (Mark 16:1-9), (2) Jesus appeared to His disciples in His resurrected body (John 20:1, 19, 26), (3) the church was established (Lev. 23:15; Acts 2:1), and (4) the church assembled for worship.

How to Observe the Lord's Day

Some want to treat the Lord's day as if it were their own day—a day for rest, fishing, or any other social activity. Others seemingly want to forbid almost anything being done on this day. Thus, the discussion of "how to observe the Lord's Day" seems relevant to our time.

The New Testament nowhere contains a passage that enumerates everything which can and cannot be done on Sunday. However, we can learn some things which the New Testament requires to be done on that day.

1. **"Break bread" (Acts 20:7).** By this phrase, I mean "to observe the Lord's Supper." When Jesus instituted the Lord's Supper, He said, "Do this in remembrance of me" (Luke 22:19). Notice that Jesus commanded Christians to observe the Lord's Supper. From Acts 20:7, we learn that the New Testament church observed the Lord's Supper on the first day of the week. Since the Supper was observed with regularity (Acts 2:42), we conclude that it was observed every first day of the week.

2. **Give (1 Cor. 16:1-2).** In these verses, Paul commanded the churches to give upon the first day of the week.

3. **Assemble with the saints (Heb. 10:25).** The author of the book of Hebrews commanded that Christians not forsake the assembly. In the assembly, of course, all forms of New Testament worship would be observed—singing, praying, giving, teaching, and breaking bread.

So far as I can determine, these are God's commandments on how the new day of worship is to be observed.

The Lord's Supper

Since the Lord's Supper is very important in New Testament worship, let us notice the following points about it:

1. **Its elements.** The elements to be used on the Lord's table are named by Jesus when He instituted the supper. He instituted the

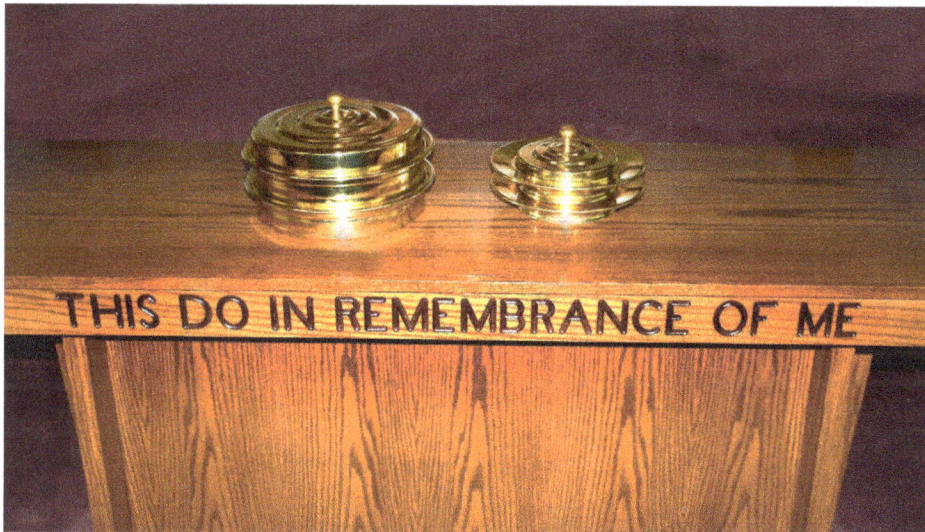

Supper during the Passover or Days of Unleavened Bread (Luke 22:1). During these days, no Jew could have leavening in his house (Exod. 12:15). Thus, we know that Jesus used unleavened bread as one element and the fruit of the vine as the other (Luke 22:19, 20).

2. Its purpose. Jesus said, "This do in remembrance of me" (1 Cor. 11:24). The Lord's Supper is a memorial to Christ and a means whereby we "proclaim His death" (1 Cor. 11:26).

Christians should be careful to observe the Lord's Supper properly since failure to do so causes one to eat and drink "damnation" to himself (1 Cor. 11:27-29). The Lord's Supper is not a common meal, but a memorial to Christ's death. Therefore, he needs to remember the Lord while partaking of it, realizing that the bread is a memorial to His body and the fruit of the vine a memorial to His blood.

Giving

Christians also need to learn to give properly. Here are some guidelines for giving:

1. Give as prospered (1 Cor. 16:1, 2). This simply means that one should give in proportion to what he makes. As one makes more, he should give more.

2. Give on the first day of the week (1 Cor. 16:1-2).

3. Give as you purpose in your heart (2 Cor. 9:7). To "purpose" means to plan one's giving. Giving is not to be done haphazardly.

4. Give cheerfully (2 Cor. 9:7).

5. Give sacrificially (Luke 21:1-4).

Conclusion

Some act as if God will not hold them accountable for not observing these acts of worship on the Lord's day. Any time that a person puts his own desires before the commandments of Christ, he has sinned. If one stays at home from worship to visit with relatives, to go on a picnic, to sleep, or to do anything else which prohibits him from observing the Lord's day, Christ has been placed second to his whims (cf. Matt. 6:33). Thus, he has placed Christ second to his earthly pleasures.

Let us always observe this new day of worship as God ordained.

Student Activities

Looking over the Lord's Supper:

1. What elements are used in the Lord's Supper? Prove your answer.

    a. _____

    b. _____

2. What does each element represent?

    a. _____

    b. _____

3. Name two purposes of the Lord's Supper.

    a. _____

    b. _____

4. 1 Corinthians 11:29 says that a person "eats and drinks judgment to himself" because he is not "discerning" the Lord's body. What does it mean to "discern" the Lord's body? You might need to consult a commentary. _____

    _____

    _____

5. On what day of the week should Christians observe the Lord's Supper? _____ Prove your answer._____

    _____

Learning More about Giving:

Below are some principles governing giving and some Bible verses on giving. Find the verse which teaches each principle and then put the letter of that principle in the blank beside the verse in which it is taught.

_____ 1. Giving on Sunday   a. Luke 21:1-3

_____ 2. Cheerful giving   b. 2 Corinthians 9:6-7

_____ 3. Giving as prospered   c. 1 Corinthians 16:1-2.

_____ 4. Sacrificial giving

_____ 5. Planned giving

In each example below, tell which principle is violated.

1. Elizabeth is given a $5.00 allowance each week. By Sunday, she has spent all of it and has nothing to put in the collection basket.

   _____

2. Roger made $50.00 this week. His mother made him put $5.00 in the collection basket even though he did not want to put in the money. _____

3. Lindsey goes to a church which takes up a collection every service, even during the week. _____

4. Steven made $200.00 this week. He gave $2.00 to the Lord.

   _____

5. Martha has been saving money to buy a new dress that costs $50.00. She had already saved $30.00 and made $20.00 babysitting this week. She decided to go ahead and buy the dress rather than give to God a part of the $20.00 she earned.

   _____

Which Day?

Given below are statements about two days of the week. Write the number of each statement in the box which fits the statement.

Sabbath Day	**Lord's Day**

1. Day on which Jesus lay in the grave.

6. The seventh day of the week.

7. Day on which the New Testament church worshipped.

8. Day on which Jesus arose from the grave.

9. Day to be observed by all nations.

10. Day on which the Israelites were not to work.

11. Day to be observed by Jews only.

12. Day on which the New Testament church was established.

Outside Activities for Presentation in Class.

1. Have someone report what "unleavened bread" is and how it is different from regular bread.

2. Have someone explain what the Corinthian church was doing wrong in observing the Lord's Supper (1 Cor. 11:23-29). Then, have him tell how we can also sin in not properly observing the Lord's Supper.

3. Have someone explain what it meant to tithe under the Mosaical law. Let him comment on whether tithing is binding on Christians and whether he thinks Christians should give more or less than the tithe.

4. Have someone prepare a talk on "Why Christians Should Partake of the Lord's Supper on Every Sunday."

The Fruit of the Lips

Lesson Objective: To show how the Christian can offer a sacrifice of praise to God with his lips.

MEMORY VERSE

"Therefore by Him let us continually offer the sacrifice of praise to God, that is, the fruit of our lips, giving thanks to His name" (Hebrews 13:15).

The Mosaical system of worship was based on a Levitical priesthood in which the worshipper had to offer praise to God through a priest. The law of Christ recognizes the priesthood of all believers (1 Pet. 2:9) and, therefore, makes possible worship without going through a priest.

The Christian is indeed commanded to "offer the sacrifice of praise to God . . . the fruit of our lips" (Heb. 13:15). Our sacrifices, according to this verse, are not burnt offerings—animal sacrifices, but is what comes from our lips. This lesson will attempt to show how our lips offer a sacrifice of praise to God.

Through Singing

One of the things commanded of Christians is singing. Through the channel of singing, the Christian can offer a sacrifice of praise to God with his lips. One of the purposes of our singing is to praise God (Acts 16:25). Hebrews 2:12 quotes an Old Testament passage to prove that Christ and Christians are brothers. But in the midst of the proof, the verse says, ". . . in the midst of the assembly I will sing praise unto You."

The ones who are "filled with the Spirit" will be "speaking to one another in psalms and hymns and spiritual songs, singing and making melody in your heart to the Lord" (Eph. 5:18-19). Hymns are songs of praise addressed to God. Thus, when the Christian sings psalms, hymns, and spiritual songs, he offers the sacrifice of praise to God.

When a person stands before the assembly while the song service is being conducted, one of the things he notices is that a large number of Christians do not sing. They fail to sing not because they cannot (a person can frequently hear them singing

secular music), but because they do not want to sing. Failure of Christians to sing indicates that they are not "filled with the Spirit."

Sometimes people sing words without their hearts being in tune with what they are singing. Such singing is merely going through the motions of worship without actually worshipping and adoring God. "These people draw near to Me with their mouth, And honor Me with their lips, But their heart is far from Me" (Matt. 15:8). A person cannot sing praise to God without "making melody in your heart" (Eph. 5:19).

When spiritual songs are sung by Christians whose spirit is striving to worship God, a sacrifice of praise, which is the fruit of our lips, ascends to God.

Through Prayer

That one can offer a sacrifice of praise with the lips in prayer is evident from the Lord's prayer. Jesus gave the example in this fashion: "In this manner, therefore, pray: Our Father in heaven, Hallowed be Your name. . . . And do not lead us into temptation, But deliver us from the evil one. For Yours is the kingdom and the power and the glory forever. Amen" (Matt. 6:9,13).

Jesus praised God with His lips in this prayer. Christians everywhere can offer the same kind of sacrifice to God; indeed, they are commanded to do just that. Christians are to "pray without ceasing" (1 Thess. 5:17).

How is your worship through prayer? Do you pray to God frequently? You need to be giving God the sacrifice of praise with your lips through prayer. Thank God for all the blessings He has given to us. Ask Him to provide for the needs that you have. Ask Him to be with the sick, the rulers of the land, and you. Thank God for Jesus, the Bible, and other Christians.

Be careful that you do not get into a rut with your prayers. When you pray, say what you feel and not what you heard someone else say. Do not say, "I pray for the sick the world over and especially the household of faith" when you mean "Father, help Mother get well." Be specific in prayer.

Through Teaching

Another means by which Christians can offer to God the sacrifice of their lips is in using their lips to teach others the gospel of Christ. Every Christian is expected to teach others about Jesus. Hebrews 5:12 contains words that indicate that the author was disgusted with a group of Christians who had not matured in faith. The author said, "For though by this time you ought to be teachers, you need someone to teach you again the first principles of the oracles of God; and you have come to need milk and not solid food."

Notice that the Christian is expected to grow in the faith to the point that he can teach others what to do to be saved. One test of the faithful Christian is the fruit test: Has he brought any fruit for Jesus? Jesus said, "If anyone does not abide in Me, he is cast out as a branch and is withered; and they gather them and throw them into the fire, and they are burned" (John 15:6).

Do you talk to your friends about Christ? Do you try to teach others what they must do to be saved? God expects you to try to teach them. Teaching others is one means by which you can offer to God the sacrifice of praise with your lips.

Offer the Sacrifice of Praise to God CONTINUALLY

The Christian is expected always to be praising God with his lips. The lips' sacrifice of praise is not something that is done only in the church building. It is to be done in daily life.

Do not pollute your altar! The altar is the place from which the sacrifice is offered. In this case, it would be your lips. You can pollute your "altar" by allowing profanity to flow from your lips. James said, "With it we bless our God and Father, and with it we curse men, who have been made in the similitude of God. Out of the same mouth proceed blessing and cursing. My brethren, these things ought not to be so" (James 3:9-10).

You can either use your lips as an altar from which you praise God or a fountain from which evil flows. The Christian will "offer the

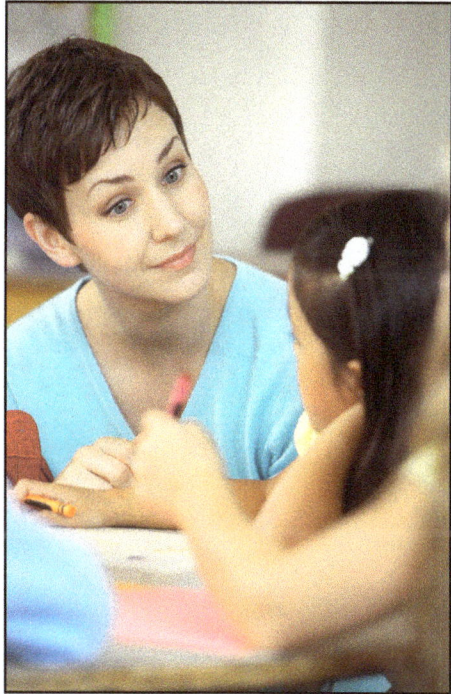

sacrifice of praise to God continually, that is, the fruit of our lips. . ."
(Heb. 13:15). "For by your words you will be justified, and by your
words you will be condemned" (Matt. 12:37).

Student Activities

Worship in Song

Match the verse to the lesson taught therein:

_____ 1. One sings when he is "filled with the Spirit."

a. Eph. 5:18-19

_____ 2. One may sing praise to God outside the assembly.

b. 1 Corinthians 14:15

_____ 3. Singing is not worship when it is not accompanied by the heart.

c. Colossians 3:16

_____ 4. Singing should praise God.

d. James 5:13

_____ 5. Singing comes from a joyful heart.

e. Acts 16:25

_____ 6. Songs are helpful in teaching fellow Christians.

f. Hebrews 2:12

_____ 7. One needs to understand what he is singing.

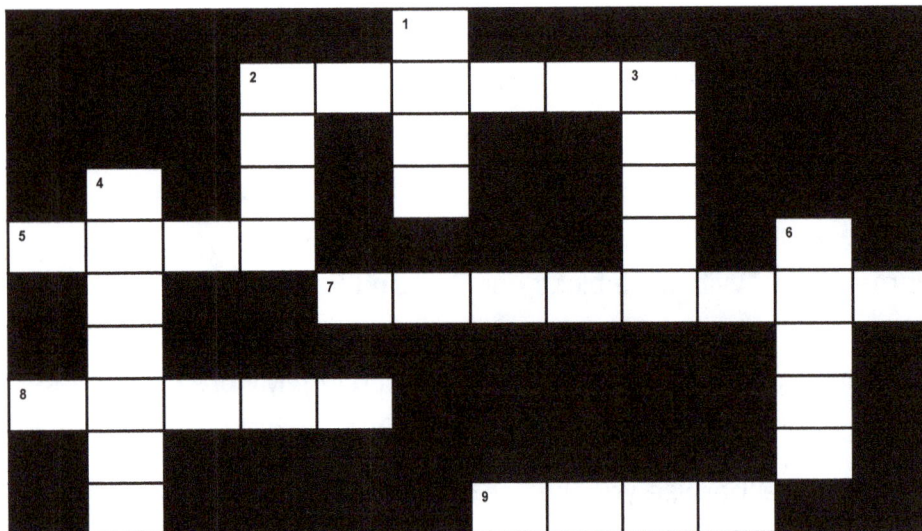

A Crossword Puzzle

Down:

1. A Christian can offer a sacrifice of praise to God with his _____ (Heb. 13:15).

2. A person must _____ without ceasing (1 Thess. 5:17).

3. The Christian is expected to grow up enough to be able to _____ others (Heb. 5:11-14).

4. A man's words will either justify or _____ him (Matt. 12:37).

6. A person should not bless God and _____ men because that is hypocritical (Jas. 3:9,10).

Across:

2. A Christian can offer worship directly to God because he is his own _____.

5. When Jesus said, "Hallowed be thy name," He meant that God's name was _____.

7. "_____ men" are the ones who teach others (2 Tim. 2:2).

8. Without one's _____ participating, worship is vain (Matt. 15:8).

9. A _____ is a song of praise to God.

Multiple Choice

_____ 1. "Worship" is best defined as (a) going to church; (b) showing reverence to God; (c) singing and praying.

_____ 2. Singing psalms, hymns, and spiritual songs is worship when (a) they are sung in the church building; (b) they are sung by many saints; (c) any person sings them from the heart; (d) all of these.

_____ 3. Teaching the gospel to the lost is the responsibility of (a) every Christian; (b) the preacher alone; (c) the preacher and elders.

_____ 4. God will recognize as acceptable worship (a) anything that is offered; (b) only that which is in spirit and in truth; (c) only that which is offered by people who live perfectly; (d) only that which is offered in the church building.

_____ 5. In prayer to God, one should (a) not be self-righteous; (b) be specific in his requests to God; (c) offer thanks for his blessings; (d) try to pray as long as possible; (e) all of these; (f) all of these except "d"; (g) all of these except "b".

Thought Questions

1. Some religions pray through the name of a patron saint or the name of Mary, the mother of Jesus. Can you find anything wrong with this practice? Prove your answer with the Scriptures.

2. Most churches use the organ and piano in worship to God. Find out the following information about their use:

   a. When were they first used in worship in the churches?

   b. Who introduced them?

   c. Does the New Testament authorize their usage?

3. Here are some approaches people use in talking to others about Christ. Discuss these approaches in class to see if any are better than the others.

   a. "John, you are, not a member of the church of Christ. Therefore, you are going to hell."

   b. "Christopher, we have known each other for a long time and have talked about many things. Will you study the Bible with me?"

   c. "You are crazy if you do not see the Bible as I do."

   d. "Both of us believe the Bible but do not agree on what it teaches. One of us is wrong. Will you go over the Bible with me to see which of us is wrong?'

4. Find three cases of conversion in the book of Acts. Name the one converted, the one preaching, and the chapter and verses of each case.

The Necessity of the Church

MEMORY VERSE

"And I also say to you that you are Peter, and on this rock I will build My church, and the gates of Hades shall not prevail against it" (Matthew 16:18).

Israelite prophets foretold the coming of a Messiah and the establishment of a Messianic kingdom centuries before Christ came to the earth. The Messianic kingdom was to be one which would never be destroyed (Dan. 2:44), include men of all nations (Isa. 2:2), be established in Jerusalem (Isa. 2:3), and be peaceful in nature (Isa. 2:4). The Jews anxiously awaited the coming of this kingdom.

"The Kingdom of Heaven Is at Hand"

When John the Baptist began his work, his message was, "Repent, for the kingdom of heaven is at hand" (Matt. 3:2). John's mission was to prepare the Israelite people for the establishment of the long predicted kingdom.

After Jesus was baptized by John, He began to preach the same message: "The time is fulfilled, and the kingdom of God is at hand. Repent, and believe in the gospel" (Mark 1:14-15). When Jesus sent the twelve apostles (Matt. 10) and the seventy disciples (Luke 10) to the cities of Israel, their purpose was to announce to Israel that the kingdom was at hand.

In one of His discourses, Jesus used the word "church" to describe the Messianic kingdom. Watch how "church" and "kingdom" are used interchangeably in these verses:

And I also say to you that you are Peter, and on this rock I will build My *church*, and the gates of Hades shall not prevail against it. And I will give you the keys of the *kingdom* of heaven . . . (Matt. 16:18-19).

Thus, whatever might be concluded about the kingdom is equally applicable to the church since they are the same thing.

The importance of the church is seen by the fact that God foretold its coming by the prophets. Also, Jesus, God's only Son, died in order that this kingdom, or church, might be established (Acts 20:28). Only in His church or kingdom can reconciliation to God occur (Eph. 2:16).

The Church and Salvation

Most religious people minimize the importance of the church. Statements such as, "You can be saved without being a member of any church," show a lack of information about the church which Jesus built.

To show the importance of the church and its relationship to salvation, one needs to lay aside his prejudice and consult only the Scriptures. Turning to Colossians 1:13-14, a person can read of Paul giving thanks to God who "has delivered us from the power of darkness and conveyed us into the kingdom of the Son of His love, in whom we have redemption through His blood, the forgiveness of sins." Notice that two kingdoms are under consideration. Every responsible person is a member of one of the two. Maybe this chart will clarify what Paul was discussing in Colossians 1:13-14.

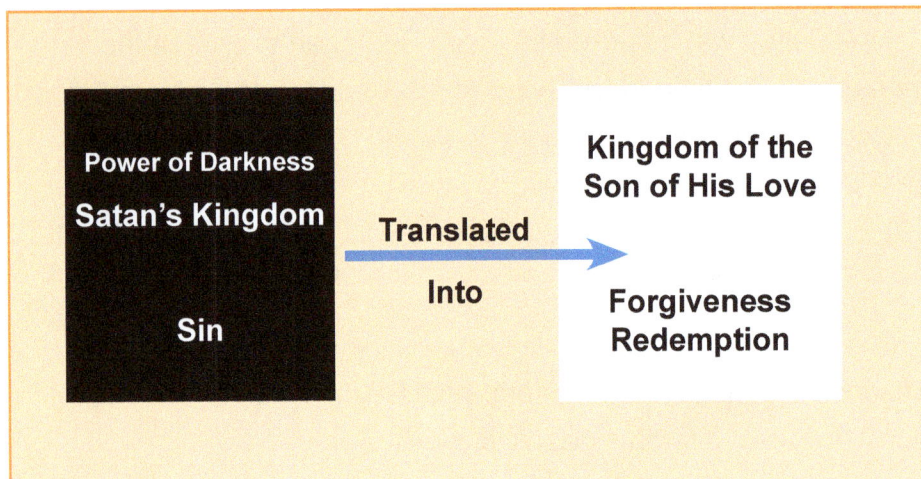

Can a person be saved while in the "power of darkness" or Satan's kingdom? Obviously not. Therefore one must be in Christ's kingdom in order to be saved. But the kingdom is the church (Matt. 16:18-19). Thus, one must be in the church which belongs to Jesus in order to be saved. Only those who have received the forgiveness of his sins are in the kingdom of God's Son

Which Church?

There are so many churches that one is confused when he decides to become a part of God's church. Which church is God's church?

Notice that Jesus only built one church (Eph. 4:4; cf. 1:22-23; Matt. 16:18—"I will build *my church*"—not churches). In His church, one can be reconciled to God by attaining the forgiveness of his sins (Eph. 2:16).

Suppose that I decided to organize a church with a certain set of peculiar doctrines. I might decide to call the church after the name of my friend Michael, the Michaelites, and emphasized the doctrines which I particularly like. If every member of our congregation decided to "join the Michaelites" and immediately became enthused to bring others into the church of the Michaelites. Before long, the Michaelites might become a large and respected church with a remarkable history for fast growth, beautiful church buildings, and helping the poor. But do we have the right to start a church? Can one be saved in a church that we might start? Can any of us die on the cross in order that all men might be saved? Obviously, the answer to all these questions is "NO!"

But if you and I have no right to start a church, what right did Martin Luther or Joseph Smith have to start a church? Don't we have the some right to start a church as they did?

That no man has a right to start a church is obvious. Since no man has the right to start a church, how can one have the hope of salvation while in a church founded by man? Salvation is available only in Christ. He expects those who are saved to work together in the church that Jesus established.

The church which Jesus established is the church which teaches and practices only what the Bible teaches. It must be patterned after the New Testament church in organization, name, worship, and work.

How to Become a Member

You must be a member of the church which belongs to Christ in order to be saved. What must you do to become a member of it? Acts 2:47 relates that God adds all the saved to Christ's church. Thus, whatever is required to be saved is what puts a person into Christ's church. The Jews on Pentecost (Acts 2) believed that Jesus was the Christ, repented of their sins, and were baptized for the remission of them (v. 38). When they did this, God added them to His church (v. 47).

You must do the same thing as they did in order to become a member of Jesus's church. Do not ever become a member of a denomination started by any man, since no man can grant salvation to you. Simply obey the gospel plan of salvation and God will deliver you from the power of darkness and translate you into the kingdom (or church) of the Son of His Love in which you can have redemption.

Student Activities
Figure out the Answers

_____ Multiply the number sent out by Jesus in Luke 10:1 by 10.

_____ Add four times the number of apostles selected by Jesus.

_____ Subtract the number of blind men healed in John 9.

_____ Add the largest number of people who saw Jesus at one time following His resurrection (1 Cor. 15:6).

_____ Add the number of men fed by Jesus in Matthew 15:38.

Place the numerals of your answer in the squares below (one number per square).

	Book of the New Testament		Chapter			Verse

Read the verse and answer the following multiple choice questions:

_____ 1. Men become members of the church by (a) joining it; (b) the church members voting them into it; (c) the Lord adding them to it.

_____ 2. The Lord adds (a) everybody; (b) all the saved; (c) all good moral men to the church.

_____ 3. The Lord added the saved to the (a) denomination of their choice; (b) the Masonic Lodge; (c) their favorite social club; (d) the church.

In Which Church?

Given below is a list of characteristics of denominational churches appearing today and characteristics of the church which Jesus built. If the characteristic is of one of denominations write "churches of men" in the blank. If the characteristic listed is of one of the New Testament church, write "church of Christ" in the blank.

1. Has pie suppers and rummage sales.

2. Has Bingo parties.

3. Teaches only the gospel.

4. Is essential to be a member of it in order to be saved.

5. Begs for money.

6. Sponsors entertainment programs.

7. Teaches that baptism is essential for salvation.

8. Uses a creed book.

Unscramble the Word

The scrambled word given below is the only thing which can be put before Jesus without a person being guilty of sin when putting it first.

HIGONTN

What is it? _____

Find the Scripture

Find the scripture which gives the answer to the following questions. Write the answer to each question and the Scripture where it is found in the blank beside each question.

Acts 20:28   **Matthew 3:2**   **Acts 2:47**
Matt. 16:18   **Ephesians 1:22-23 Romans 16:16**

1. Who is the Head of the Church? _____

2. How may one become a part of the church? _____

3. What purchased the church? _____

4. Give one of the names for the church. _____

5. Who said, "Repent, for the kingdom of heaven is at hand"? ____

    _____

6. Who said, "I will build My church"? _____

Outside Assignments

1. Find out by whom, when, and where the Seventh Day Adventist church was founded.

2. Contrast what the Baptist Church and the Bible teaches about the purpose of baptism.

3. Conduct a survey of non-members of the church of Christ to see how many believe that being a member of the church is essential to salvation. Ask at least two people.

4. Write out a script in which a Christian talks with a non-Christian about the relationship of the church to salvation. Make the scene open with the non-Christian saying, "I do not have to be a member of any church in order to go to heaven."

The Organization of the Church

Lesson Objective:
To describe the universal and local organization of the New Testament church and to contrast that with the organization of some denominations.

MEMORY VERSE

"And He put all things under His feet, and gave Him to be head over all things to the church" (Ephesians 1:22).

If the church unorganized, confusion prevailed, God disapproves of disorder and confusion (1 Cor. 14:33, 40). Therefore, the church of Jesus Christ is an organized institution.

Organization of the Universal Church

Some offices in the church are limited in authority to the local congregations; other offices are unlimited in scope and include authority over all congregations. These offices have authority over the church universal. They are as follows:

1. Jesus Christ: "head over all things to the church" (Eph. 1:22). Jesus, following His resurrection, said, "All authority has been given to Me in heaven and on earth" (Matt. 28:18). Jesus is the person who possesses all authority in the church; He is the king in His kingdom. Notice that the organization of the church is not democratic or a republic, but is monarchial. Jesus is the monarch with all power.

2. Apostles: ambassadors on behalf of Christ (2 Cor. 5:20). The apostles were commissioned by Jesus to go into all the world. They were given the authority to "bind and loose." Jesus told all of the apostles, ". . . whatever you bind on earth will be bound in heaven, and whatever you loose on earth will be loosed in heaven" (Matt. 18:18). The apostles revealed and bound on men what God expected them to do in order to be saved; they also loosed Jews from the bondage of the Mosaical law. Their statements of revelation applied to all men and not to just the members of one local church.

3. Prophets. Prophets not only foretold the future, but also revealed the mind of God on a variety of subjects. Like the apostles, they were able to give God's will on a particular subject. What they revealed applied to all congregations.

Paul said that the "household of God" had "been built on the foundation of the apostles and prophets, Jesus Christ Himself being the chief cornerstone" (Eph. 2:20).

The words of the Lord, apostles, and prophets are in our New Testaments. Today, we have no living apostles or prophets whose authority extends to all congregations. Rather, the authority of the Lord is revealed to men through His written word.

Organization of the Local Church

Inside the local church, some offices are given to govern that local church. Paul named all of the offices in the local church when he opened his letter to the church at Philippi with the following words: "Paul and Timothy, bondservants of Jesus Christ, To all the saints in Christ Jesus who are in Philippi, with the bishops and deacons" (Phil. 1:1). Here are the offices in the local church:

1. **Elders (Acts 14:23).** The elders are also called *bishops* or *overseers* (Acts 20:17, 28; Titus 1:5, 7) and *pastors* (Eph. 4:11). The work of the elders is (a) to oversee the congregation and rule it (1 Pet. 5:2; 1 Tim. 5:17); (b) to watch over the flock (Acts 20:28); (c) generally, to make all the provisions necessary to take care of the souls in their care (Heb. 13:17).

The authority of the elders is limited to the local church. They are to "tend the flock of God which is among you" (1 Pet. 5:2). Elders of a local church have authority over the church of which they are members. They have no authority over any other church.

The members of a local church are supposed to submit to the elders so long as the elders are in obedience to God's commandments (Heb. 13:17).

2. **Deacons.** The word translated "deacon" (*diakonos*) means "one who renders service to another." The deacon is a man especially charged by the church to perform services for the church. Acts 6:1-6 records the case of some men appointed by the Jerusalem church to distribute alms for the church. A deacon might be charged to take care of the treasury, maintain the building, attend to the needs of the elderly, or be sure that the communion is prepared. These men work under the elders.

3. **Saints.** All of the rest of the members are simply saints. Included in the ones working under the elders is the preacher. He

should never be called "pastor," unless he is also an elder, since the word "pastor" is used in the Bible to describe the elder.

The qualifications of the elder are listed in 1 Timothy 3:1-7 and Titus 1:5-9; the qualifications of a deacon are recorded in 1 Timothy 3:8-13. Elders should be appointed as soon as they are qualified. However, no unqualified man should be appointed as an elder. A church can be scriptural in organization if it has no elders, so long as no men are qualified. The churches which Paul established on his first missionary journey existed for at least a year before elders were appointed in them (Acts 14:23). Thus, we learn that to have no elders is better than to have unqualified men usurping the office of an elder.

Perverted Church Organization

Denominations have perverted the organization of the church by adding offices over the universal church. Here is an outline of the organization of two denominations:

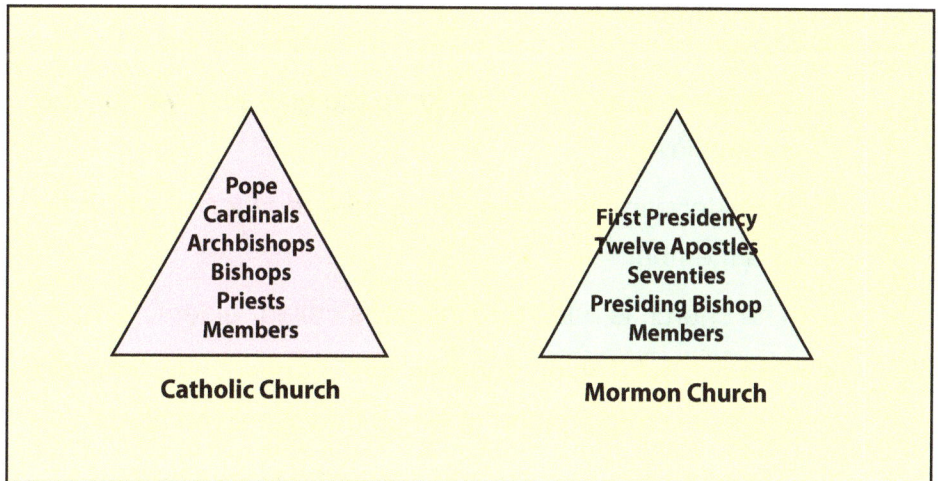

Pope
Cardinals
Archbishops
Bishops
Priests
Members

Catholic Church

First Presidency
Twelve Apostles
Seventies
Presiding Bishop
Members

Mormon Church

Notice that offices other than the Bible offices are added to the organization of these denominations. No Bible authority can be given for these offices.

Some churches of Christ also pervert the organization of the church by making the elders of one church oversee the work of another church. Sometimes a church becomes a "sponsoring church." This term in not found in the Bible, but it is sometimes used to describe an organization which requests all churches to contribute money to one church which then oversees the spending of the monies contributed by hundreds or thousands of churches. The elders of the "sponsoring church" have taken authority over a work of more than one church when they take charge of the spending of funds for many churches. This is a perversion of the organization of the local church.

Conclusion

By knowing the scriptural organization of the church, a person is better equipped to identify the church which Jesus built. He can ask a particular denomination to outline its organizational structure and contrast that with the organization revealed in the New Testament to see if that particular body is a church belonging to the Lord. Too, he is better prepared to work in a local church when he knows how and by what authority the local congregation is organized as it is. Let Christians learn to be content with the organization given by Jesus to govern His church.

Student Activities
True or False

_____ 1. The work of an elder is to keep the grass mowed on the church lawn.

_____ 2. An elder can oversee only the congregation of which he is a member.

_____ 3. The church is ruled by monarchs called "elders."

_____ 4. The authority of the apostles and prophets was limited to the local congregation of which they were members.

_____ 5. The work of a deacon is to oversee the members of a local congregation.

_____ 6. A man twenty years old could hold the office of on elder.

Problem Churches!

1. The church where John attends wants to help preach the gospel in China. They have decided to write to all the churches in the United States to ask them to send money to their elders who will then send the money to preachers in China. What is wrong with this organizational arrangement?

2. The church where Jason attends does not have any elders. At present, the congregation has one man fully qualified. Another man is qualified in all but one point. What should the church do?

3. The church where Linda attends has three qualified men serving as elders. The church decided to send $500 a month to support a preacher in another state. Since Linda does not want the church to support the preacher, she decides to contribute her money to another congregation. Did Linda do anything wrong?

Whose Work?

Match the work and office. Some have more than one answer.

a. **Jesus**   d. **Elders**

b. **Apostles**   e. **Deacons**

c. **Prophets**   f. **All Saints**

_____ 1. To reveal God's plan of salvation.

_____ 2. To teach God's plan of salvation.

_____ 3. To oversee the local congregation.

_____ 4. To have unlimited authority or "all power."

_____ 5. To keep the financial records of a local church.

_____ 6. To be sure that the needs of the poor are met.

_____ 7. To discipline the disobedient in the flock of God.

_____ 8. To submit to the elders.

Home Assignments

1. Have someone call a denomination to find out how it is organized.

2. Discuss the limits of the authority of the elders of a local congregation.

3. What does it mean for the elders to be "lords over those entrusted to you" as described in 1 Peter 5:3?

The Work of the Church

Churches across the land have misunderstood their primary purpose for being in existence if the activities in which they engage are any indication of what they understand to be the purpose for the church. Some churches have become money-making institutions, others have become welfare service organization, some have become schools and day-care centers, and still others have become recreational centers. Thus, we need to learn what works God expects the church to accomplish.

If we can learn in what works the early church were engaged and duplicate them, we can rest assured that we are doing the works which God has assigned for the church. Paul commended the church at Thessalonica for becoming followers of the churches of God in Judea (1 Thess. 2:14). We likewise should imitate the approved examples cited in the New Testament as works of the church.

The Work of the Church

1. **To build up its members.** One of the works of the early church was that of leading the members toward spiritual maturity. The elders of the church at Ephesus were instructed to "take heed to yourselves and to all the flock, among which the Holy Spirit has made you overseers, to shepherd the church of God which He purchased with His own blood" (Acts 20:28). The elders had the responsibility to feed the church in order to educate it in the Scriptures, to prevent false teachers from destroying the flock.

Unless this work of leading the new converts to maturity is accomplished, none of the other works that God has given the church to do will be accomplished.

The work of perfecting the saints is not always easy to accomplish. Some of the means by which the church seeks to accomplish this task are Bible study, sermons, and gospel meetings. By imparting Bible knowledge to the saints, each man is made more aware of what God expects of him. He is taught how being a

Lesson Objective:
To show what is the work of the church as well as to point out some things which are not the work of the church.

MEMORY VERSE

"The things which you learned and received and heard and saw in me, these do, and the God of peace will be with you" (Philippians 4:9).

"saint" affects his daily life. Participation in Bible study and gospel meetings is essential for the accomplishment of the perfecting of the saints.

2. To help the needy saints. The early church pooled its resources to help the needy saints. When cases of necessity arose, the saints had "all things in common." Some members even sold their property in order to feed the poor (Acts 4:32-37).

As a congregation, the members have a responsibility only to the saints. (In every passage which discusses the church helping the poor, those who were helped were saints or Christians.) As individuals, the members have a responsibility to all men, but especially to fellow saints. Read our individual obligations as recorded in the following passages: "Therefore, as we have opportunity, let us do good to all, especially to those who are of the household of faith" (Gal. 6:10); "Pure and undefiled religion before God and the Father is this: to visit orphans and widows in their trouble, and to keep oneself unspotted from the world" (Jas. 1:27).

Thus, the second work which the church as a collective body has to accomplish is to take care of its own needy families. Then, as individuals, the members of the church are to do as much as possible to help needy families who are not members of the church.

3. To preach the gospel to all the world. The Great Commission orders the apostles to "go into all the world, and preach the gospel to every creature" (Mark 16:15). Paul called the church "the pillar and ground of the truth" (1 Tim. 3:15) because it supported the proclamation of the gospel.

Thus, a third work of the church is to support gospel preachers while they spread the gospel to the world (2 Cor. 11:8; Phil. 4:15-16; 1 Cor. 9:14). Gospel preaching is done through weekly sermons, gospel meetings, radio broadcasts, printed materials, and house-to-house preaching. This work of spreading the gospel is not limited to preachers.

The individual Christian is told this: "And the things that you have heard from me among many witnesses, commit these to faithful men who will be able to teach others also" (2 Tim. 2:2). No Christian is discharging his responsibilities to God unless he has enough concern to teach the lost.

These three works are the only works which God has given the church to accomplish. However, man has become discontent with the works which God has given the church to accomplish. Consequently, churches have become involved with works other than these God-given works.

Works in Which the Church Should Not Engage

1. **Recreation.** Churches are involved with recreation to such an extent that the church begins to look like a social club. Providing softball games, teen outings, youth camps, etc. is not the work of the church. Clean recreation is not sinful, but the parents, and not the church, are the ones responsible for providing it for their children.

2. **Business.** Many denominations supplement their income by going into business for profit. Honest businesses are not wrong, but the work of the church is not to build apartments for rent, to sell clothes, to make tires, etc. The income of the church is supplied by the freewill offerings of its members.

3. **Universal benevolence.** Some churches try to assume the role of taking care of the poor of the world. In the New Testament, the churches never tried to take care of all the poor in the world but only the poor among the saints. Only individually, as one has the opportunity, does the church have responsibility to the world. The work of the church is not to provide hospitals, old folks homes, orphans homes, etc. for all the world.

4. **Secular education.** Some churches of Christ, as well as denominations, operate schools and support colleges from their treasury. The church, has no responsibility to teach math, science,

engineering, agriculture, history, etc. The obligation to educate children belongs to the parents.

5. Day-care. The church is not in the business of providing day-care services for working parents.

6. Politics. Though not a few preachers and churches have tried to take active parts in the politics of our country, the work of the church is not involved with the political issues of the day. Jesus was never distracted to speak about the evils of dictatorial government, slavery, and high taxation. To say that the church should not become involved in politics is not to minimize the importance of political issues. Rather, to show that the church should not be involved in these affairs is to recognize the proper sphere in which the church should work.

Conclusion

The work of the church is threefold: (a) to edify and perfect the saints; (b) to relieve the needs of the poor among the saints, and (c) to preach the gospel to all nations. Any works other than these, however good they may be, are not the works of the church.

In identifying the church which Jesus established, knowledge of what is the work of the church is important. A person can check to see if a certain church is involved in activities other than the ones given above. If it is, that church is not the New Testament church which was established by Jesus,

Student Activities
Whose Work Is It?

Below is a list of works which need to be accomplished. In the two boxes below, one is labeled "work of the church" and the other is labeled "work of the individual." Put the number beside each work into the proper box. Some works might go into both boxes.

Work of the Church	Work of the Individual

1. To support the American Cancer Society.

2. To preach the gospel.

3. To support the county little league.

4. To provide groceries for my neighbor who is not a member of the church.

5. To build a college in which to educate Christian's children.

6. To build an orphans' home to take care of all the orphans in the world.

7. To provide classes to teach Christians how to live pleasing to God.

8. To support a Christian woman who has no income.

9. To build apartments to be leased to old folks.

10. To build a hospital in an under-developed country.

11. To provide day-care services for working parents.

12. To provide secular education in a Christian environment.

How Should the Need Be Met?

1. John is a Christian who was raised by Christian parents. Recently, his father died and left his mother without any means of support. Read 1 Timothy 5:3-16 and tell how this godly woman should be supported. _____

2. Scott and Jennifer are members of the church. Their house was recently destroyed by fire. What should be done to help them? What is the responsibility of the members of the church as individuals and as the church?_____

3. A family in town was in a car wreck which killed the parents and orphaned two children. What should be done to support the children? _____

Multiple Choice:

_____ 1. The work of the church is (a) to evangelize the whole world; (b) to take care of the physical needs of all the world; (c) to build and support hospitals and colleges.

_____ 2. Providing recreation is (a) the work of the church; (b) no one's obligation since recreation is sinful; (c) the responsibility of parents.

_____ 3. A church which becomes involved in works other than those given in the Bible is (a) to be commended for rendering service above and beyond the call of duty; (b) sinful for going beyond what the Scriptures authorize.

_____ 4. A church can support a college if (a) a well-known preacher said that it could; (b) all the elders agree to support it; (c) the Bible authorizes it.

Short Answer:

1. Tell how the church can discharge its responsibilities in each of these areas:

   a. Edifying the saints: _____

   b. Helping the needy: _____

   c. Evangelizing the world:_____

2. The local Baptist church sponsors a softball team each summer. Is anything wrong with that practice? If so, what? _____

   _____

3. One denomination owns an apartment complex, a shopping center, a clothing factory, and other things. Is this right or wrong? How is the church to raise money? _____

   _____

4. Since many Christians forsake the assembly, read Hebrews 10:24-25. From that passage discuss what the Christian should do to help "perfect the saint" who is forsaking the assembly. ____

Workers in the Church

God detests laziness! In Proverbs, the wise man wrote, "As vinegar to the teeth and smoke to the eyes, So is the lazy man to those who send him" (10:26). Though that verse was written with regard to physical work, we know that the same is true of spiritual work in the church because Paul admonished Christians to be "not lagging in diligence; fervent in spirit; serving the Lord" (Rom. 12:11).

In another verse, Paul said, "For we are God's fellow workers" (1 Cor. 3:9). Christians have the privilege of being allowed to work with God in works He has given the church to accomplish.

"What can I do?" Not knowing what to do might be the only thing that is keeping you from doing any work for the Lord. In this lesson, we will try to help you see some of the works which God expects each Christian to accomplish. Before discussing the works which God expects Christians to perform, I must point out that, first of all, you must be living faithfully to God. I mean that you should be living a pure life and attending worship regularly. Assuming that you are already doing these things, let us study what works a Christian should do.

Teach the World

The primary work which God has given the church to accomplish is "to teach all nations" (Matt. 28:19). In accomplishing this work, the church employs several methods, including the following: radio broadcasts, bulletins, pulpit preaching, etc. In none of these can teenagers be very active at the present. (Check to see if you can help fold and address the bulletin, if the congregation with which you work publishes one.) But these are not the only methods through which the world is taught.

When the church was persecuted in Jerusalem, the saints fled from that city to other places. Luke, the historian, said, "Therefore they that were scattered abroad went everywhere preaching the word" (Acts 8:4). Every saint taught someone else.

Lesson Objective: To show that God expects every Christian to be zealous of good works.

MEMORY VERSE

". . . Looking for the blessed hope and glorious appearing of our great God and Savior Jesus Christ, who gave Himself for us, that He might redeem us from every lawless deed and purify for Himself His own special people, zealous for good works" (Titus 2:13-14).

Here is where you can begin to work. You, as a Christian, can teach someone else what to do to be saved. God expects every Christian to become a teacher in order to spread His gospel. In the book of Hebrews, the author became disgusted with several Christians because they did not grow enough in the faith to become teachers. Therefore, he wrote, "For when for the time ye ought to be teachers, ye have need that one teach you again which be the first principles of the oracles of God; and are become such as have need of milk, and not of strong meat" (Heb. 5:12).

What kind of Christian will you become—one who grows in the faith in order to teach others or one who will always be in need of being taught. God expects you to be a teacher. Will you become a teacher?

How many of your friends need to be taught the plan of salvation? If you do not teach them, who will? If you do not teach them, what chance do they have of reaching heaven?

General Works

In order for the church to exist, a certain amount of work has to be done. Some of the works that must be performed are simple and easy enough for you to do them; other jobs are so hard that even the elders find them difficult.

The young men who are Christians can begin to lead in public prayer, pass the communion, lead singing, usher people into the assembly, and do other works in the assembly. Outside the assembly, the young men can help do the physical work of keeping the property looking presentable. (For example, a young man could keep the yard mowed.)

There are also works for young women to do. Most of the things listed as works for the boys are not open for girls to perform. However, there are areas in which the young woman can excel which are not open to men. A young woman can cook food to take to a sick or needy family, help clean the church building (dusting, mopping, or sweeping), prepare the communion, assist the teachers in Bible class for smaller children, etc.

Most of the works which have been named thus far in the lesson are probably being done by the ones in the church who should be out teaching the gospel in a public manner or in home Bible studies. Acts 6:1-6 teaches that every member should do what he can in order that the ones qualified to teach publicly do not become entangled in less important activities.

Planning Your Life

What do you plan to do in life? Do you plan to be a doctor or a nurse, a lawyer or a school teacher, a policeman or a secretary? In planning your life, do not forget God!

Young men should plan to devote their lives to the work of the Lord. Some could be preachers, others could be elders, and still others could be deacons. However, these works, like the professions mentioned above, require preparation and planning. If you want to do any of these works which God expects of Christians, you must study and grow in the knowledge of the word of God.

Young women should also plan to give their lives to God. Some preacher, elder, or deacon will need a godly woman to stand by his side. The church will always need teachers to work with the children. These tasks are open for you, but they will require preparation and work.

Right now, you could ask your teacher to help you find out what works you can do in the church. In closing this lesson, read this poem which points out that each of us has a job to do:

Room in God's Kingdom

There is room in the kingdom of God, my brother,
For the small things that you can do;
Just a small, kindly deed that may cheer another
Is the work God has planned for you.

Just a cup of cold water in His name given
May the hope in some heart renew;
Do not wait to be told, nor by sorrow driven
To the work God has planned for you.

There's a place in the service of God for workers
Who are loyal to Him and true;
Can't you say to Him now, "I will leave the shirkers,
And the work Thou hast planned I'll do."

There is room, there's a place,
In the kingdom of God for you;
There is room, there's a place,
There is work that we all can do.

J. R. Baxter, Jr.

Student Activities
Multiple Choice

_____ 1. The apostles in Acts 6:1-6 did not want to serve tables because (a) they were too good to do that kind of work; (b) they needed to be preaching the gospel and could not quit preaching in order to do this less important job; (c) they were not interested in that kind of work.

_____ 2. Teaching is a job for (a) every Christian; (b) the elders and preachers; (c) only the men of the congregation.

_____ 3. A young man should (a) cross his fingers and hope that some day he may be qualified to be an elder or a deacon; (b) not worry about God's work since he is young only once in life; (c) plan his life so that he can be prepared to serve God as a preacher, elder, or deacon.

_____ 4. A young woman (a) cannot do anything in the work of the church since men do it all; (b) should plan to develop into a godly Christian woman who teaches classes, helps the sick, etc.; (c) not worry about God's work since she is young only once in life.

_____ 5. A person who does not have time to work in the church but has time to engage in all forms of recreation is (a) putting Christ second in his life; (b) not necessarily a weak member of the church; (c) living in such a way as to get the most out of life.

True or False

_____ 1. The work of the church is to be done by the elders, deacons, and preachers.

_____ 2. God expects you to learn enough to be able to teach others the gospel.

_____ 3. The little jobs which you can do are so unimportant that no one cares, least of all God, whether or not you do them.

_____ 4. Laziness among Christians in performing good works is unexcusable.

_____ 5. Not knowing what to do is one of the causes of people doing nothing in service to God.

Crossword Puzzle

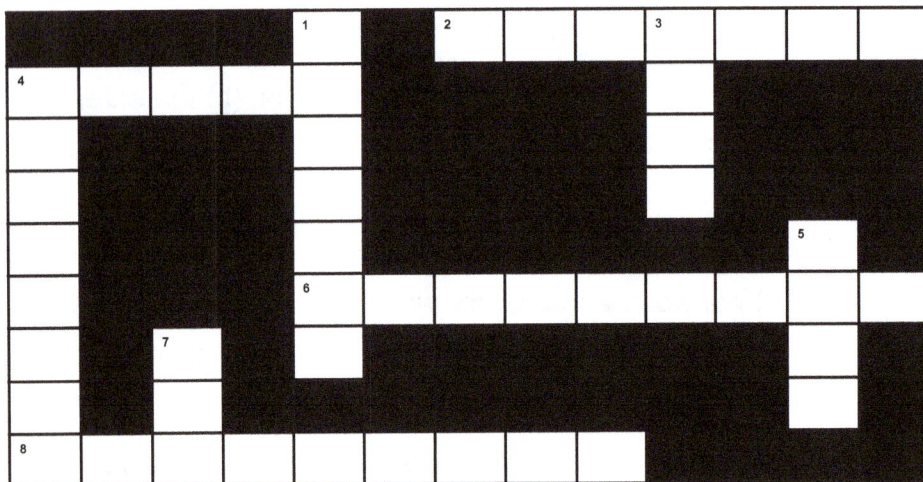

Across:

2. God's people should be _____ of good works" (Titus 2:14).

4. The apostles did not want to "leave the word of God and _____ tables" (Acts 6:2).

6. "No one engaged in warfare _____ himself with the affairs of this life, that he may please him who enlisted him as a soldier" (2 Tim. 2:4).

74

8. "And we desire that each one of you show the same _____ to the full assurance of hope until the end, that you do not become sluggish, but imitate those who through faith and patience inherit the promises" (Heb. 6:11, 12).

Down:

1. After a period of time, every Christian should become a _____ (Heb. 5:13).

3. "If you _____ me, keep my commandments" (John 14:21).

4. "Go to the ant, you _____! Consider her ways and be wise" (Prov. 6:6).

5. A person's faith is _____ if it does not make him perform the works God has commanded (Jas. 2:14-17).

7. _____ Christians should teach the gospel.

Some Work Projects:

1. Call the sick and tell them that you missed them at worship services.

2. See if you can help with the mailing of the church bulletin or the cleaning of the building.

3. Talk to your friends and relatives about obeying the gospel of Christ or becoming more faithful to Him.